ORACLE OF GOD
Devotional
JAN - JUNE 2016

© STEVIE OKAURU

Published by: MAHP
Interior Design by: Mark Asemota, MAHP USA
Cover Design by: Mark A. H SpiritWorkz Graphics
Editing by: Stevie Okauru
Creative Consultant: Mark A. H SpiritWorkz

Copyright © 2015 by Stevie Okauru
All rights reserved. This book or any portion thereof may not be reproduced or used in any manner whatsoever without the express written permission of the publisher except for the use of brief quotations in a book review.

Printed in the United States of America

This Paperback Edition First Printing, 2015

ISBN-13:978-1-62676-975-5

Mark Asemota House of Publishing [MAHP]
535 Pensacola Dr,
Maryland, MD 20878

For wholesale ordering or further enquiries please visit www.oogod.org

The Moral right of the Author has been asserted

PRESENT TO

_____

_____

*To Him who is Worthy
of Our Devotion*

New year edition!

SWORD WORD
OF THE ORACLE

ORACLE OF GOD DEVOTIONAL SERIES
BY REV STEVIE OKAURU

INTRODUCTION

First and foremost I thank the Holy Spirit for the newly redesigned and optimized Oracle of God Devotional subtitled 'TREASURE OF HEAVEN'. This internationally acclaimed and favorite daily devotional has been re-enhanced and optimized for a quicker, stronger and faster spiritual growth and development.

In addition to the prophetic words from on high and deliverance prayers; I've included in this edition, inspiring, and revelational basic Hebrew words study and systematic Sunday School lessons every week for your edification. With these special features, you would learn and understand certain key Hebrew words; their imports, implications and connotations in scriptures and life applications.

The renewed version of this devotional; will definitely position you for daily victory and uncommon success as you imbibe life-changing thoughts in this edition. You'll not only be refreshed, you'll also be completely transformed!

Remember! Your problems are not the biggest thing in your life. Jesus is. Serve Him with your thoughts and He will set you free! Matthew 6:24-25 say "Ye cannot serve God and mammon. Therefore I say unto you, Take no thought for your life...." See also Isaiah 55; 2 Corinthians 10:5. Jesus Christ is Lord!

Apostle Stevie Okauru
[Founder and Overseer OGIM]

INTRODUCTION USING THIS BOOK FOR MAXIMIZED IMPACT AND UTMOST IMPARTATION

I. Diligently read and meditate on the day's scripture[s]!

II. Declare and claim severally the Word of Prophecy for the day!

III. Diligently meditate on the short 'revelational' message, as you pray and confess aloud the confessions/declaration!

IV. Read through the assigned Bible passage of "THE BIBLE IN ONE YEAR"

V. You may read the Old Testament portion in the morning and the New Testament Portion at night.

VI. You can also use "THE BIBLE IN ONE YEAR" reading plan to prayerfully plan, write down, your daily, weekly and monthly goals and objectives. Thereby measure your progress and success as your scale one hurdle or obstacle after the other.

VII. I personally invite you to come and experience God's love and glorious presence in one of our worship Tabernacles and on our prophetic and deliverance prayer conference daily @ 302.202.1110 enter 605815 at the prompt or 712.432.0071 and enter 188641# at the prompt. @ 6-7am and 10-11pm Eastern Standard Time. Apostle Stevie Okauru; Ministering!

OTHER HELPFUL HINTS!

Most scripture quotation in this book is from the New King James Version [NKJV] Bible except otherwise indicate.

KEYS FOR OTHER BIBLE VERSION USED

Here are some abbreviations of Bible Versions in use:

The Earliest Bibles

- **DSS** = Dead Sea Scrolls, *remains of an ancient Jewish library, written in Hebrew, Aramaic, and Greek. The library includes Hebrew Bible manuscripts, as well as Apocrypha and other Jewish literature of the period. (2nd cent. B.C. - 1st cent. A.D.).*

- **LXX** = Septuagint *(the Greek version of the Hebrew Bible, translated by Jewish scribes between 250-100 B.C., which included the Apocrypha)*

- **Elpenor** = Bilingual LXX *with English translation of L.C.L. Brenton (1851)*

- **LXX 2012** = *Septuagint in American English 2012 (1885, 2012)*

- **NETS** = New English Translation of the Septuagint.

- **MT** = Masoretic Text *(the traditional text of the Hebrew Bible, which may be dated to Rabbi Akiva's efforts to standardize the Hebrew canon in the early 2nd century A.D. Extant MSS only date to the 10th cent. A.D.)*

- **S** = Syriac *(the Bible in Syrian Aramaic; the Tanakh was first translated by Jews, probably Messianic Jews, in the late 1st century to early 2nd century, and the Besekh [THE NEW TESTAMENT] by Christians in the late 2nd century.*

- **T** = Targums, *Aramaic translation of the Tanakh [THE OLD TESTAMENT] with interpretative comments (Extant MSS dated to 70-135 A.D., although such translation existed in an oral form a long time before that, which Jewish authorities date to the time of Ezra.)*

- **V** or **Vul** = Biblica Sacra Vulgata, Jerome *(the Latin version of the Bible, A.D. 405)*

- **Early English Versions of the Bible** *(Public Domain)*

- **Bishop** = The Bishop's Bible (1568).

- **Coverdale** = Coverdale Bible, Miles Coverdale.

- **GNV** = The Geneva Bible (1587).

- **KJV** = King James Version, *known in Britain as the Authorized Version (1611; revised 1769; based on the TR).*

- **Mace** = New Testament in Greek and English, *Daniel Mace (1729).*

- **Tyndale** = Tyndale New Testament, *William Tyndale (1526).*

- **Wesley** = The New Testament, John Wesley (1790).

- **WYC** = Wycliffe Bible, John Wycliffe (1395).

Greek Texts of the Besekh

TR = TextusReceptus ("Received Text", 1633 ed. of Erasmus' Greek text of 1516). This Greek text is the basis for the KJV. Online (1894 ed.)

WH-Text = The New Testament in Greek, B.F. Westcott & F.J.A. Hort (1881; incorporated reading of newly discovered early manuscripts) Online

Maj-Text, M-Text = Majority Text (AKA Byzantine Text; consists of the largest number of surviving manuscripts, though not the oldest.) NKJV uses the abbreviation M-Text.

NA21-28 = NovumTestamentumGraece. ed. Eberhard Nestle, Erwin Nestle, Kurt Aland, et. al. American Bible Society and the British and Foreign Bible Society. (NA1, 1898; NA13, 1927; NA21, 1952; NA25, 1963; NA26, 1975; NA27, 1993; NA28, 2012). This Greek text incorporates the reading of the earliest manuscripts and is generally followed by modern Bible versions. The differences between editions are largely the textual apparatus added listing variant readings of interest to translators and Greek Scholars.

UBS1-4 = The Greek New Testament. ed. Kurt Aland, Bruce Metzger, et. al. United Bible Societies. (UBS1, 1966; UBS2, 1968; UBS3, 1975; UBS4, 1993; UBS3 and UBS4 correspond to NA26.)

NU-Text = *Abbreviation used in the New King James Version to denote the combined reading of the Nestle-Aland Greek New Testament (N) and the United Bible Societies' Greek New Testament (U).*

Hebrew Versions of the Besekh

- **BSI-NT** = Ha'BritHa'Chadashah [New Covenant]: TirgumChadash. [New Translation]. Bible Society in Israel, 1991. Online. (Modern Hebrew)

- **Delitzsch** = Franz Delitzsch (1813-1890), *Hebrew New Testament.* Leipzig, 1877. (Biblical Hebrew)

- **DHE** = Franz Delitzsch (1813-1890). *The Delitzsch Hebrew-English Gospels. Vine of David,* 2011. (Hebrew with English translation)

- **HEB** = Hebrew-English Bible. *The Bible Society in Israel and the Israel Association for the Dissemination of Biblical Writings, 1996. (Modern Hebrew with English NKJV)*

- **Margoliouth** = Ezekiel Margoliouth, *Ha'BritHa'Chadashah al pi Mashiach [New Covenant of the Messiah] Public Domain, 1927.* Online. (Biblical Hebrew)

- **Salkinson** = Isaac E. Salkinson (1820-1883) and Christian D. Ginsberg (1831-1914), *Ha-Berit ha-Hadashah.* British Missionary Society, 1886. Online. (19th c. Hebrew)

Modern English Versions of the Bible (post 1800)

- **ABP** = The Apostolic Bible Polyglot, *Charles Van der Pool (2006)*. *An interlinear of the Greek Tanakh, with English translation. Online. Download.*

- **AMP** = The Amplified Bible, *The Lockman Foundation (1987)*.

- **ASV** = American Standard Version (1901).

- **BBE** = The Bible in Basic English, *C. K. Ogden*.

- **BRV** = Holy Bible, English Revised Version *(1881)*. *[British revision of KJV]*

- **CEB** = Common English Bible, *Common English Bible (2011)*.

- **CEV** = Contemporary English Version, *American Bible Society (1995)*.

- **CJB** = Complete Jewish Bible, *David Stern (1998)*. *[Messianic Jewish version]*

- **Darby** = Darby Bible, J.N. Darby (1890).

- **DHE** = Franz Delitzsch (1813-1890), *TheDelitzsch Hebrew Gospels. Vine of David, 2011.* (Citation of "DHE" indicates the English translation provided by the publisher.)

- **DRA/DRB** = Douay-Rheims Bible, *American Edition*.

- **Einspruch** = Henry Einspruch, *The Good News According to Matthew. Lederer Publications, 1964.* *[Messianic Jewish version]*

- **EMTV** = *English Majority Text Version: New Testament, translation.* Paul W. Esposito (2009).

- **ERV** = Easy-to-Read Version, *World Bible Translation Center (2006)*.

- **ESV** = The English Standard Version, *Crossway Bibles (2001)*.

- **EXB** = The Expanded Bible, *Thomas Nelson Inc.*

- **GNC** = God's New Covenant: *A New Testament Translation*, Heinrich Walter Cassirer (1989). *[Jewish Christian version]*

- **GNT/GNB/TEV** = *Good News Translation,* American Bible Society (1992); formerly known as Today's English Version (1976).

- **Goodspeed** = Edgar J. Goodspeed, *The New Testament: An American Translation (1923)*.

- ***GW*** = God's Word, God's Word to the Nations.

- ***HCSB*** = Holman Christian Standard Bible, *Holman Bible Publishers (2003)*.

- ***HEB*** = Hebrew-English Bible, *The Bible Society in Israel (1996)* [Parallel Bible with both Tanakh and Besekh in Hebrew with NKJV English text.]

HNV = Hebrew Names Version of the World English Bible, Michael Paul Johnson (2008). [Messianic Jewish translation] AKA Messianic Edition of the World English Bible. Online.

JB =Jerusalem Bible, Darton, Longman & Todd (1966). [Roman Catholic]

JPTR =Judaica Press Tanach with Rashi Commentary

JPS =The Holy Scriptures According to the Masoretic Text, Jewish Publication Society of America (1917).

JUB = Jubilee Bible, Life Sentence Publishing.

KJ21 = 21st Century King James Version, Deuel Enterprises, Inc. (1994).

Knox = Knox Bible, Westminster Diocese (2012).

TLB = The Living Bible, Kenneth Taylor (1971).

Lamsa = The Holy Bible from Ancient Eastern Manuscripts, ed. George M. Lamsa (1985) (translation of the Aramaic Old and New Testaments)

LEB = Lexham English Bible, Logos Bible Software.

LITV = Literal Translation of the Holy Bible, J.P. Green (1976). Online.

- **ME-WEB** = Messianic Edition of the World English Bible, Public Domain (2008). See **HNV**.

- **MLB** = Modern Language Bible: The New Berkeley Version in Modern English, Zondervan Pub. House.

- **Moffatt** = A New Translation of the Bible, James Moffatt (1926).

- **Mounce-NT or MRINT** = Mounce Reverse Interlinear New Testament, Robert H. Mounce and William D. Mounce (2011).

- **MSG** = The Message: The Bible in Contemporary Language, E. H. Peterson (2002).

- **M** = The Messianic Writings, Daniel Gruber (2012). [Messianic Jewish version]

- **NAB** = The New American Bible, USCCB (1986). [Roman Catholic] Online.

- **NABRE** = The New American Bible, Revised Edition, USCCB (2011). [Roman Catholic]

- **NASB, NAU** = New American Standard Bible, Lockman Foundation (1960, 1962, 1963, 1968, 1971, 1972, 1973, 1975, 1977; Updated Edition 1995).

- **NCV** = New Century Version, Thomas Nelson, Inc.

- **NEB** = The New English Bible (1970). Online.

- **NET** = The NET Bible/New English Translation, Biblical Studies Press (2005).

- **NETS** = New English Translation of the Septuagint.
- **NIRV** = New International Reader's Version, Biblica, Inc. (1998)
- **NIV** = The New International Version, Biblica, Inc.
- **NJB** = New Jerusalem Bible, Doubleday Religion (1999). [Roman Catholic]
- **NJPS** = New Jewish Publication Society of America Version of the Tanakh (1985).
- **NKJV** = New King James Version, Thomas Nelson, Inc. (1982).
- **NLT** = New Living Translation, Tyndale House Foundation (1996, 2007).
- **NLV** = New Life Version, Christian Literature International (2006).
- **NOG** = The Names of God Bible, Baker Publishing Group (2011).
- **NRSV** = New Revised Standard Version, Division of Christian Education of the National Council of the Churches of Christ in the United States of America.
- **OANT** = The Original Aramaic New Testament in Plain English with Psalms & Proverbs (8th edition), Glenn David Bauscher (2013).
- **OJB** = Orthodox Jewish Bible, Phillip Goble, Artists for Israel International. [Messianic Jewish Version].
- **Phillips** = The New Testament in Modern English, J. B. Phillips (1958).
- **PLT** = Peshitta: Lamsa Translation (George Lamsa, Holy Bible: From the Ancient Eastern Text, 1957; Revised 1985).
- **REB** = Revised English Bible (1989).
- **RSV** = Revised Standard Version, Division of Christian Education of the National Council of the Churches of Christ in the United States of America.

WWW.OOGOD.ORG/

- **RSV-CE** = Revised Standard Version, Catholic Edition (1966, 2006).
- **RV** = Revised Version (NT 1881; OT 1885).
- **TEV** = See GNT above.
- **TLB** = The Living Bible, Kenneth Taylor (1971).
- **TLV** = Messianic Jewish Family Bible: Tree of Life Version, Messianic Jewish Family Bible Society (2014). [Messianic Jewish version] Online.
- **TNIV** = Today's New International Version, Biblica, Inc. (2005).
- **Voice** = The Voice Bible, Thomas Nelson, Inc.; Ecclesia Bible Society (2012).
- **WE** = Worldwide English New Testament, SOON Educational Publications (1969, 1971, 1996, 1998).

WEB = World English Bible, trans. Michael Paul Johnson (1997).

WMB = World Messianic Bible, trans. Michael Paul Johnson (2014); aka Hebrew Names Version **(HNV)**. Online.

- **WEY or Weymouth** = Weymouth New Testament, Richard Francis Weymouth (1903).

103. **YLT** = Young's Literal Translation, *Robert Young*.

WWW.OOGOD.ORG/

DONATE@ORACLEOFGODMINISTRIES.NET

take the
SWORD
of the SPIRIT which is the
Word of God.
[EPHESIANS 6:17]

January 1st

[ONE YEAR BIBLE PLAN: Genesis 1-3/ Matthew 1]

Today's Word: Psalm 103:1-22

I DECREE! GREATNESS ON ME AS I PRAISE GOD!

Happy New Year! Congratulations!

Saint! Everything you do this year, do it with all your might! You can learn from a shepherd boy that became the greatest king Israel ever had. Everything David did, he did vigorously. At war, he fought with all his might. When he praised and danced for God, even as a king, no one could beat him at it. Why not start this year with praising God like never before and your life will never remain the same in Jesus' name!

GIVE QUALITY PAISE TO THE ALMIGHY GOD!

Father God! I bless Your Holy Name! King of Kings and Lord of lords I praise You! The I Am that I Am; I worship You! Ancient of Days! Alpha, and Omega, the Beginning, and the Ending, the Almighty God, Wonderful, Counselor, Mighty God, Everlasting Father, Prince of Peace! Glory to Your Holy Name! Thank You for the New Year! Thank You for years gone! In Jesus' name I worship. Amen!

JANUARY BIRTHDAY AND WEDDING PRAYERS!

Lord I commit all Your children born in the month of January into Your hand; I commit also, all the marriages consummated this month to You; For the rest of their lives, let them be the first and not the last; let them be head and not tail. Anoint them, bless prosper empower and let them enjoy marital bliss in Jesus' name. Amen!

January 2nd

[ONE YEAR BIBLE PLAN: Genesis 4-6/Matthew 2]

Today's Word: 2 Kings 13:3

*"Then the **anger** of the Lord was aroused against Israel, and He delivered them into the hand of Hazael king of Syria, and into the hand of Ben-Hadad the son of Hazael, all their days."*

ANGER [HEBREW] 'APH

'Aph is the Hebrew word for 'anger' as used in the above text-verse and also in [Deuteronomy 6:15; Proverbs 29:8] Strong's Concordance #639. Depending on the context, this word signifies either 'nose' or 'nostril,' or 'anger' [Genesis 2:7; Proverbs 15:1]. About half of the time of the occurrence of this term: it is associated with words referring to burning. Thus, these figures of speech typically depict 'anger' as the fierce breathing of a person through his nose: 'a burning nose' [Exodus 32:10-12].

Most of this word reference, describes God's 'anger'. He is said to be slow to 'anger', but can be provoked into exercising judgment [Psalm 103:8; Deuteronomy 4:24-25]. The Lord is compassionate, but His wrath is reserved for those who break His Covenant [Deuteronomy 13:17; Deuteronomy 29:25-27; Joshua 23:16; Judges 2:20; Psalm 78:38]. Although God's wrath is righteous, because His 'anger' is a reaction to unrighteousness; human 'anger' is almost always evaluated in negative terms in the Old Testament [Genesis 49:6; Proverbs 14:17].

Prayer: Father Lord! Deliver me from the spirit of anger!

First Sunday of the Month of January

[ONE YEAR BIBLE PLAN: Genesis 7-9/ Matthew 3]

CHURCH AND HOME SUNDAY SCHOOL

JESUS CHRIST INSTRUCTED HIS DISCIPLES TO BAPTIZE 'IN THE NAME OF THE FATHER, THE SON AND THE HOLY GHOST'.

Why then do they baptize in the name of Jesus Christ?

They followed Jesus Christ's command to baptize in the name of the Father, the Son and the Holy Ghost by baptizing, the New Testament believers in the name for the 'Triune God'- 'Lord Jesus Christ'. Triune name is tri-unity God. LORD: The JHVH of the Old Testament. JESUS: the earthly name, the name of His humanity; CHRIST: The name of the Spirit, the anointing, the Messiah.

Acts 2:37-38 *"Now when they heard this, they were cut to the heart, and said to Peter and the rest of the apostles, "Men and brethren, what shall we do?" Then Peter said to them, "Repent, and let every one of you be baptized in the name of Jesus Christ for the remission of sins; and you shall receive the gift of the Holy Spirit."*

WHAT IS THE DIFFERENCE BETWEEN THE BAPTISM OF JOHN AND THE BAPTISM OF JESUS CHRIST?

John the Baptist's baptism was a baptism of repentance and preparation for the Messiah. It shows that those who had been baptized by him had repented of their sins; were looking forward to the Messiah. It was an outward act declaring their repentance. Christ's baptism, was also a baptism of repentance, it is an inward work for

the circumcision of the heart and an entrance into Christ and an initiation into the New Covenant.

Acts 19:3-4 *"And he said to them, "Into what then were you baptized?" So they said, "Into John's baptism." 4 Then Paul said, "John indeed baptized with a baptism of repentance, saying to the people that they should believe on Him who would come after him, that is, on Christ Jesus."*

Sunday School Questions

1) Why do they baptize in the name of Jesus Christ?
2) What is the difference between the baptism of John and the baptism of Jesus Christ?

> **Memory Verse:** Acts 2:38 "Then Peter said to them, "Repent, and let every one of you be baptized in the name of Jesus Christ for the remission of sins; and you shall receive the gift of the Holy Spirit."

Prayer

1) Lord! I thank you for the provision of Baptism into Your Body in the name of Jesus. Amen!
2) Every satanic influence in me is quenched by fire in the name of Jesus. Amen!
3) Every anointing of demonic Baptism in my life is canceled by the blood of Jesus.
4) Lord, deliver me from the spirit of ancestral error! Thank God for Prayer answered

January 4th

[ONE YEAR BIBLE PLAN: Genesis 10-12/Matthew 4]

Today's Word: Psalm 90:12

I DECREE! I WILL NOT WASTE TIME THIS YEAR!

This New Year 2016 may seem very long now, but it takes wisdom to see the whole from the parts. If you live for 70yrs; and this is split into phases; Childhood phase would take the first 13yrs. If you sleep 6hrs daily for 70yrs; that takes 17 yrs; the remaining 40 yrs involve schooling, work, leisure, religious activities etc. The reality is that you've far less time at your disposal than you thought. Splitting years into days gives you room to appreciate life; it helps you to maximize potentials, and enable you to re-prioritize. You then know what is truly important and what is merely essential. This year 2016, you must invest times not spend it. King Solomon says, *"Teach me to number my days, that I might apply my heart to wisdom."* Wisdom here requires that you increase your time with God in comparison with other things this year. Ephesians 5:16 says: *"... redeeming the time for the days are evil."* This means that, having lost so many years to Satan while you were a in the world, you have to now optimize the time left for God's glory. Let every minute count this year. Outline your goal and break it down, with set targets of what you plan to achieve in 6 months, quarterly, monthly, weekly and daily. Work to meet the daily requirement while keeping the week in focus. Doing this with prayer can help you accomplish your goal this year. Trim off hours of sleep; increase your time with the Lord. Pay your daily 2.4 hrs tithe of time in worship, prayers, witnessing etc. Plan your days for success! And I prophesy you will not waste time this year in Jesus' name!

January 5th

[ONE YEAR BIBLE PLAN: Genesis 13-15/Matthew 5:1-24]

Today's Word: 2 Kings 3:10-14

I DECREE! PEOPLE SHALL GREATLY HONOR ME!

Solomon said in [Ecclesiastes 7:1]. (CEV) In Life a good reputation at death is better than loving care at the time of birth. In our text-passage above; the King of Israel, the king of Judah and the King of Edom went to Elisha for divine direction out of their frustration and predicament. On arrival, Elisha gave, King Joram of Israel, a shocker of his life. Elisha was resolved not to help. Elisha, who is a subject of the king of Israel, refused to aid his own king. But when Jehoshaphat king of Judah, pleaded with the prophet; Elisha honored Jehoshaphat. Considering the reputation and status of King Joram of Israel and that of King Jehoshaphat of Judah, you would without doubt agree that a good name and reputation is better than might and wealth. Whereas, Jehoshaphat ruled over Judah which was one out of the twelve tribes of Israel; Joram was king over the remaining eleven tribes.

So, obviously, Joram was richer and more powerful. Yet, because of his bad reputation, he was worth nothing before God. There are so many people like that today. They've achieved a lot in life; money, power, position and might etc. Yet their reputation does not command any respect whatsoever. Are you one of such people? I admonish you to repent, return to God for you own good. And people will honor you henceforth in the name Jesus. Amen!

Prayer: Father Lord! Make me honorable all the days of my life in Jesus' name. Amen!

January 6th

[ONE YEAR BIBLE PLAN: Gen. 16-17/Matthew 5:25-48]

Today's Word: Romans 8:28

I SHALL FULFILL GOD'S PURPOSE FOR MY LIFE!

The Lord is a God of purpose. And believe it or not He has a great purpose for you than you may realize. You must move further than rejoicing for being saved. You must know that there is a greater purpose for you than just being saved. Our text-verse above says there is a great call upon your life; not just to get out of Egypt and be free of satanic clutches, but also with an object of the fullness of Son-ship; the fullness of being a bon-a-fide child of God. It is great that we are called into Christ, but how many are really in their calling; and if we think we are in our calling; do we really know for sure? Are we experiencing the meaning of it; if indeed we are in it?

Saint! Are you one of those who are not walking according to the purpose or calling of God upon their lives? Are you spiritually unfulfilled? Do you hunger for more of God? Do you hunger for that which you are called to be and to do? I prophesy! As the Oracle of God, you shall now begin to operate in your divine call in Jesus' name! You must know you are not called just to be saved; just to get to heaven, and have the blessings of life that comes with salvation.

You must know that their lies before you and within your reach an awesome purpose of God for you. 1 Corinthians 2:9 say *"...Eye has not seen, nor ear heard, nor have entered into the heart of man the things which God has prepared for those who love Him."* Do you love God? Pray thus:

Prayer: Lord Jesus! Empower me to walk in my calling!

January 7th

[ONE YEAR BIBLE PLAN: Genesis 18-19 /Matthew 6:1-18]

Today's Word: 2 Kings 6:1-7

I DECREE! ALL MY LOST OPPORTUNITY SHALL SWIM TO ME THIS YEAR!

I decree this day, that the Holy Spirit will empower you to grab your restored opportunities. In 2 Kings 6:1-7 is the story of the sons of the prophet who went cutting down wood and the axe-head they borrowed for the task fell into the river. They were blessed with wives, and with kids, so their accommodation became too small for them. And they had the opportunity to build for themselves; bigger and better accommodation, but they lost the means to achieving their aim in river Jordan. *I pray! The evil river swallowing your resources shall vomit it now in Jesus' name. Amen!* But then, by the power of the anointing on Prophet Elisha, the Oracle of God, the iron was brought back to the surface. The lost opportunity was restored. But more than that, the iron didn't just come to the surface; it literally swam to them; for God knew that none of them could swim. Saint! God knows your limitations, and He sent me to get you out of that limitation, He knows the system has placed you in a category but this day, I come to de-categorize you in the name of Jesus!

The Bible said the axe head began to swim like a fish until the one who needed it stretched forth his hand and picked it up. I decree by the decree of heaven! Your lost opportunities, and resources will beckon to you and you shall surely grab it!

Prayer: I command all my lost opportunity be restored to me this time in Jesus' name. Amen!

January 8th

[ONE YEAR BIBLE PLAN: Gen. 20-22 /Matthew 6:19-34]

Today's Word: Psalm 32:1-2; 2 Samuel 6:6-7

I DECLARE! GOD'S ANGER SHALL NOT BE KINDLED AGAINST ME!

The more I think of it; the more I am at lost on why Uzzah suffered the fate he suffered. We understand from scripture that Uzzah tried to steady the Ark of God to prevent it from falling. By human standards, that act was actually a noble and commendable deed indeed. But for whatever reason, he died instead of been blessed for a seemingly good and noble deed. He fell on the wrong side of God's judgment scale: The bible says "the anger of the LORD was kindle against Uzzah, and God smote him for his error: and he died by the ark of God". What a strange fate! But that only further proof God's sovereignty. Therefore, no one can question His deeds and decisions. He determines who He shows mercy and who not to show mercy. Like Uzzah, David erred. But the anger of God was not kindled against him. That is why David was a passionate advocate of the mercy of God [Psalm 32]. As humans, it is almost impossible not to err. But the difference between those who are destroyed and those who get a second chance; is of the mercy of God and nothing else. *I pray that God's anger will not be kindled against you in Jesus' name.* As the Oracle of God, I prophesy the mercy of God upon you, and your loved ones in Jesus' name. Amen!

Prayer: Lord! Have mercy on me and my family always in the name of Jesus. Amen!!

January 9th

[ONE YEAR BIBLE PLAN: Genesis 23-24 / Matthew 7]

Today's Word: 2 Kings 14:4

"However the high places were not taken away, and the people still sacrificed and burned incense on the high places."

HIGH PLACE [HEBREW] 'BOMAH'

The Hebrew word for 'high place' is 'Bomah' as used in the above passage and also in [2 Kings 23:5; 1 Kings 11:7; and Jeremiah 19:5] Strong's Concordance #1116: This word often refers to a sacred area, or place, or an open-air sanctuary, located on a ridge.

Before the temple was built, the Children of Israel could worship the true God at high places: like Solomon's worship of God at the 'high places' in Gibeon, in [1 Kings 3:2-4]. But the Israelites soon began worshipping other gods, especially Baal, at such 'high places', imitating the practices of their neighboring nations.

They decorated these hilltops with pagan symbols, sacred pillars and stones, and these places were rallying points for pagan worship. They often were associated with Israel's religious rebellion and apostasy [1 Kings 14:23; Jeremiah 19:5]. So, throughout the Old Testament, the existence of 'high places' and the worship that was practiced there was labeled as an affront to the Almighty God. Psalm 78:58 *"For they provoked Him to anger with their 'high places', and moved Him to jealousy with their carved images."*

Prayer: Lord! Purge my heart of any idolatry in Jesus' name!

Second Sunday of the Month of January

[ONE YEAR BIBLE PLAN: Gen. 25-26 / Matthew 8:1-17]

CHURCH AND HOME SUNDAY SCHOOL

What did the people do; who received John's baptism?

When they heard of the baptism of Jesus Christ, they were re-baptized in the name of the Lord Jesus Christ. Acts 19:5 *"When they heard this they were baptized in the name of the Lord Jesus."*

IS IT POSSIBLE TO BE BAPTIZED AND NOT RECEIVE A CIRCUMCISED HEART?

Yes! To receive a circumcised heart, the Holy Spirit must prepare the heart by giving us the desire and the faith to be born again. When baptism is not preceded by heart preparation, it is merely a rite and not an experience.

Hebrews 4:2 *"For indeed the gospel was preached to us as well as to them; but the word which they heard did not profit them, not being mixed with faith in those who heard it."*

2 Corinthians 3:6 *"who also made us sufficient as ministers of the new covenant, not of the letter but of the Spirit; for the letter kills, but the Spirit gives life."*

Sunday School Question

1) What did the people do; who received john's baptism?
2) Is it possible to be baptized and not receive a circumcised heart?

Memory Verse: Acts 19:5 "When they heard this, they were baptized in the name of the Lord Jesus."

January 11th

[ONE YEAR BIBLE PLAN: Gen. 27-28 /Matthew 8:18-34]

Today's Word: Ruth 2:1-10

I DECREE! A SUDDEN MIRACLE UPON MY LIFE THIS SEASON!

When the scripture said; the path of the righteous is directed by God, it is referring to such situations as in the above passage. Ruth left the house that morning; without having any idea of where the next meal would come from. She told Naomi, her mother in-law, that she would simply go to any field and see if they would allow her glean [search for left-over grain for food] for their up-keep. But Lo and Behold the Lord God eventually led her to a place where she was not just allowed to glean grains for that day, but she was given access to come daily for her daily provision. A classic case of divine provision you may say! I pray, you receive divine provision from unexpected quarters this month in Jesus' name. Amen!

By coming in contact with Boaz, Ruth did not only step into divine provision; but unknowingly, she stumbled upon a lifetime miracle; her future husband; and entered the lineage of Our Lord and Savior Jesus Christ [Matthew 1:5]. What are you seeking right now? Is it divine connections, provisions, or favors? Are you unaware of how you will make ends meet? Cheer up Saint, because the Spirit that led Ruth to her miracle is here to guide you also. Just be alert and you will receive a sudden miracle in the name of Jesus. Amen!

Prayer: I will experience divine provision from unexpected quarters this month in Jesus' name. Amen!

January 12th

[ONE YEAR BIBLE PLAN: Genesis 29-30 /Matthew 9:1-17]

Today's Word: Genesis 39:1-22

I DECREE! DIVINE FAVOR AND MERCY UPON MY LIFE!

Joseph experienced divine favor at the hand of God amidst hideous conspiracy, false accusation and adversities. And that is what is called uncommon favor or grace. In spite of the entire sad occurrences in Joseph's life, his life story ended on a glorious note because of the favor of God upon him.

In the text-passage above, Portiphar's wife lied against Joseph resulting in his wrongful imprisonment without any set date of release. Humanly speaking, that seemed to be the end of Joseph and His dreams. But that was not to be as because "...God was with Joseph...and gave him favor....." in and out of prison. *I pray for you this day that the Lord will grant you and your love ones uncommon favor in Jesus' name. Amen!*

Consequently, Joseph prospered in slavery. Beloveth! Your life may have been a terrible story of persecutions and accusations; you may be experiencing unusual and unhealthy rivalry in your work place and household. You may have been suffering and laboring under a generational curse for a protracted period of time.

I come now to decree upon you; by the decree of heaven the favor of God! I decree by heavens authority that your prosperity shall come forth mightily and speedily; off your adversity, in Jesus' gracious name. Amen!

Prayer: O God bring upon me, uncommon favor and mercy!

January 13th

[ONE YEAR BIBLE PLAN: Gen. 31-32 /Matthew 9:18-38]

Today's Word: Deuteronomy 6:18-23

I DECREE! THE CRISIS OF MY LIFE SHALL BECOME A TESTIMONY!

The deliverance of the children of Israel from Egypt is their greatest testimony ever; because of the enormity of the attended miracles, signs and wonders; especially the dividing of the Red Sea. But, their suffering in Egypt was horrible; it was a period enslavement, with the greatest humiliation and degradation ever. But, that period was also preceded by testimonies wherein they used their mouths to recount the mercies of the Lord upon them. You must never resign to fate but hold on to God's Word and promises in dignity. As you hope on God for a change of circumstance. Know that every difficulty; has within it, a seed of testimony waiting to germinate and produce results. So, if you are facing any difficulty now, do not lose hope just yet; don't begin to think that the whole world is unfair to you; that life is unfair to you.

Life is just preparing you for a great testimony. If the problem is very big, expect a big testimony. You are due for a miracle. You may not believe this; because of your present situation; but no matter how unpalatable your condition is right now; just be prepare for a pleasant surprise from God! As you look onto Him beyond your issues in faith, the crisis of your life shall become testimonies in Jesus' name! The same God who turned around the captivity of Israel into testimony will visit you this time of your life in Jesus' name. I declare in the name of the Lord you are next in line to testify. Alleluia!

January 14th

[ONE YEAR BIBLE PLAN: Gen. 33-35 /Matthew 10:1-20]

Today's Word: Isaiah 40:1-5

"Comfort, yes, comfort My people!" Says your God. "Speak comfort to Jerusalem, and cry out to her, that her warfare is ended........"

THE LORD GOD SHALL COMFORT ME!

Isaiah 40:3-4 *"The voice of him that crieth in the wilderness, Prepare ye the way of the LORD, make straight in the desert a highway for our God. Every valley shall be exalted, and every mountain and hill shall be made low: and the crooked path shall be made straight and the rough places plain:"* I prophesy; every crooked path of your destiny shall be straightened now in the name of Jesus Christ. Amen!

Crooked paths connote areas of your live that are not functioning according to God's will for you. For instance, you may have all the good things of life; but, you are not healthy due to one health issue or other; so that defect is your own crooked path. You may be healthy, wealthy and famous but you may not be able to get married; that is your own reproach, it is a crooked path. Some people are married but have no children. Some have one child/one gender syndrome. All these unfulfilled desires constitute crooked paths in people's lives. Some can't find emotional and spiritual fulfillment in life that also is a crooked path; a reproach in their life. Crooked paths are sources of sorrow in people's lives. *I prophesy the crooked path in your life is straightened this day in Jesus' name. Amen!*

Prayer: Every crooked path in my life is straightened now in the name of Jesus. Amen!

January 15th

[ONE YEAR BIBLE PLAN: Gen. 36-38 /Matthew 10:21-42]

Today's Word: Romans 3:27

THE LAW OF FAITH SHALL WORK FOR ME!

If you work the Word, the Word will work for you. The same way the law of gravity operates in the physical; so also the law of faith is; in the spirit realm. A law is a constant and works for anyone, everyone, everywhere, anywhere, anytime and every time under the right circumstances. Gravity, as a law functions always. That is the reason we don't find ourselves floating as we walk along the way. The law of gravity is what keeps us on the ground. In the same vein, the law of faith can be counted on; to work at all times. There are no trials and errors with established laws; laws don't forgive, they either work for you or against you. The law of faith will work for you or against you, depending on how you relate to it. Try to use your faith, for faith always works; if it is faith then it has already worked.

The scripture define faith as the evidence of things not seen [Hebrews 11:1]. If something is evidence it means it is proof of something that already exists. So, if for instance, somebody who is sick of cancer declares in faith *'I am healed in Jesus' name; the cancerous growth in my body is dead!'* Now, if what that person has is really faith, it means the growth is actually already dead though he may still feel or see the problem with his/her physical eyes.

When you understand that faith is a law, it helps you: firstly, to know if what you thought was faith was really faith. Secondly, it gives you the confidence to know that faith always works! That means you can stake your life on it; since it is a law that works for everyone that applies it rightly! Glory to God!

January 16th

[ONE YEAR BIBLE PLAN: Genesis 39-40 /Matthew 11]

Today's Word: 2 Kings 17:7

"For so it was that the children of Israel had sinned against the Lord their God, who had brought them up out of the land of Egypt, from under the hand of Pharaoh king of Egypt; and they had feared other gods."

DOING WRONG [HEBREW] 'CHATA'

The Hebrew word 'Chata' is rendered 'wrong doing' or 'doing wrong' as in our text-verse above and also in 2 Kings 18:14; Leviticus 4:27-28; Judges 20:16; Strong's Concordance #2398. The meaning of this verb is 'to miss [a target] or to miss [a mark]' or 'to fall short [of a goal].'

The word expresses this basic meaning in [Judges 20:16], where it is translated miss: 'not everyone could sling a stone at a hair' breathe and not miss.' When applied to ethics, the word implies falling short of moral requirement.

The word is the most common Old Testament expression for sin. Several nouns are derived from the verb, including Chet' [sin of guilt] [Isaiah 53:12], Chatta' 'sinful men' [Numbers 32:14] and Chatta't 'sin offering' [Leviticus 4:3]. In the New Testament, Paul also defined sin as 'falling short': "for all have sinned and fall short of the glory of God." [Romans 3:23]. But then, Paul offered the perfect remedy for our fallen condition: salvation through Jesus Christ. [Romans 3:24]

Prayer: Lord Jesus! I thank you for the provision of salvation!

Third Sunday of the Month of January

[ONE YEAR BIBLE PLAN: Gen. 41-42 /Matthew 12:1-23]

CHURCH AND HOME SUNDAY SCHOOL

What to do if our baptism was only a rite?

If our baptism was merely a rite, we must ask the Holy Spirit to prepare us for the promised experience. When we have the assurance that the heart is fully prepared, we should be baptized. 1 Corinthians 12:13 *"For by one Spirit we were all baptized into one body—whether Jews or Greeks, whether slaves or free—and have all been made to drink into one Spirit."* See also Ephesians 4:4-5

WHAT IS THE SECOND BAPTISM WE MUST EXPERIENCE? The Holy Spirit: Acts 2:38

WHAT IS THE BAPTISM IN THE HOLY SPIRIT? The baptism in the Holy Spirit is an empowering for service that takes place after the experience of salvation. It enables us to witness to the Lord's salvation and to demonstrate one or more of the nine gifts of the Holy Spirit. Just as the indwelling Spirit reproduces the life of Christ, the outpoured Spirit reproduces the ministry of Jesus Christ on earth. Acts 1:8

Sunday School Question

1) What should we do if our baptism was only a rite?
2) What is the second baptism we must experience?
3) What is the baptism in the Holy Spirit?

> **Memory Verse:** Acts 1:8 "But you shall receive power when the Holy Spirit has come upon you; and you shall be witnessesto Me in Jerusalem, and in all Judea and Samaria, and tothe end of the earth."

January 18th

[ONE YEAR BIBLE PLAN: Gen. 43-45 /Matthew 12:24-50]

Today's Word: 2 Chronicles 1:6-11

I DECREE! I SHALL RECEIVE AN OPEN CHECK THIS YEAR!

There are certain actions you can take this year 2016 that can provoke the blessings of God upon your life. And top of the list is sacrificial giving. Solomon is one man that understood and applied this principle in his life. And that enabled him to become the richest and the wisest king of Israel. In [2 Chronicles 1], Solomon broke all records of giving; when he offered a thousand burnt offerings to God at Gibeon. And obviously impressed by the enormity of that sacrifice, God appeared unto Solomon and gave him a blank check to choose whatever he wanted. Solomon asked for wisdom, which consequently opened the gates for his extra-ordinary greatness, fame and wealth. I decree by the decree of heaven that your sacrificial giving will provoke uncommon breakthroughs for you and your loved ones in Jesus' name!

Beloveth, have you been sowing into the kingdom for a long time without adequate recompense? Have you offered yourself as a living sacrifice unto the Lord your God; and yet your situation has not changed? Or are you still expecting the harvest for sown seeds? Hear now the counsel of God, this season, the Lord will grant you a blank check. I decree, you shall receive an open check in Jesus' name. Amen!

Prayer: Lord! I am open to receive all the blessings that You've released unto me in Jesus' name. Amen!

January 19th

[ONE YEAR BIBLE PLAN: Gen. 46-48 /Matthew 13:1-30]

Today's Word: Deuteronomy 2:29-34

I DECREE! EVERY TEMPEST CONTRIVED AGAINST ME IS DESTROYED!

In spiritual phraseology, 'Sihon' means tempest; while 'Heshbon' means contrivance: figuratively and summarily speaking, Sihon King of Heshbon connotes tempests that are contrived by the devil to hinder the progress of God's people.

When Satan and His cohorts saw the speed at which Moses and the Israelites were cruising through the desert, they contrived to present Sihon, a man whose emotions, might and power is likened to the tempest to hinder them. In accordance to his nature, Sihon mounted a tempestuous opposition against the children of God. But the Lord God empowered Israel to ride and glide over the tempest; as they overcame Sihon.

These days, tempest rises in all forms and sizes to disrupt people's progress in life. They come in the form of threats, financial difficulties, health and marital issues etc. When tempest comes; they come in torrents bringing one problem after the other until the victim is demoralized and stagnated. Saint! Are you facing such tempest in life? Are you dealing with siege-like tempest contrived against you by household or workplace wickedness? Hear the Word of the Lord this day! You are empowered to overcome and over run your negative situation in the name of Jesus Christ. Amen!

Prayer: I overrun and overcome every tempestuous situation in my life in the name of Jesus Christ. Amen!

January 20th

[ONE YEAR BIBLE PLAN: Gen. 49-50 /Matthew 13:31-58]

Today's Word: Nehemiah 2:1-9

GOD WILL BRING ME UNTO UNCOMMON FAVOR!

Indeed, there is no limit to which God can go to satisfy the desires of those who diligently seek to do His will: Nehemiah's story attests to this.

Ordinarily, a position as exalted as an aide to the king of the powerful Persian Empire would have been more than enough for any slave. But not for Nehemiah; when he heard of the sufferings of his people in Jerusalem, he took his career and his life in his hands and spoke to the king requesting permission to go and rebuild the city of David. At that time, it was grand treason to try, or even suggest rebuilding the city of Jerusalem, which is a vassal state of the Persian kingdom. Yet, not only did Nehemiah ask for permission, he also place demands on the king in [Nehemiah 2:7] to give him consignment for the assignment. Strangely, and against all odds, Nehemiah had all his requests granted because he found favor with the king. As the Oracle of God I decree your grand return this season in Jesus' name. Amen!

Saint! I don't know what you're going through right now; neither does it matter what the odds are that are against you: I prophesy today; you will find favor with men in high and low places in Jesus' name. Amen! Henceforth, I implore you to be more involved in Kingdom works. As you do so, the God of Nehemiah will take you higher in the name of Jesus. Amen!

Prayer: O God bestow upon me uncommon Favor!

January 21st

[ONE YEAR BIBLE PLAN: Exodus 1-3 /Matthew 14:1-21]

Today's Word: Nehemiah 2:1-9

I WILL FIND FAVOR WITH THE KING OF KINGS!

Have you a sad countenance? Do you have an unfulfilled feeling because of situations around you? Do you feel unsatisfied with life because you are unable to assist those in need? I want you to cheer up because your sad story is about to change for good! Nehemiah had the same issue; he was a slave in a strange land with others. Those who were left behind in Jerusalem were suffering all kinds of afflictions. And he could not do anything about it as it were. But one day, God stepped into the situation: and since God can't come down Himself to help anyone; He made Nehemiah find favor with king Artaxerxes. And consequently, the king provided Nehemiah with everything he needed to help his people.

Saint! Do you desire to help the helpless? Do you have the desire to help solve problems around you? I decree as the Oracle of God! You will find favor with God and with man, the King of kings will divinely favor you in Jesus' name! As you burn with the desire to aid humanity, the God of Nehemiah would surely aid you to accomplish your heart's desire in Jesus' name. Amen! From now on, men and women, white and black, great and not so great shall bring you blessings in the Jesus' name. As you go about your life, I pray that the God of Nehemiah be with you in Jesus' name. Amen!

Prayer: I command the angel of God to bring me favor with all sundries in Jesus' name. Amen!

January 22nd

[ONE YEAR BIBLE PLAN: Exodus 4-6 /Matthew 14:22-36]

Today's Word: Psalm 37:23

I WILL BE DIVINELY LED TO MY DESTINY HELPER!

It would be a great declaration if you did declare the above decree severally and with resounding Amen! This is because the declaration is far more important than many other attributes of success. In His wisdom; God has already pre-arranged the route of success for all His children. For every individual, He has positioned someone to help them at every stage in life. These people are destiny helpers. Until you discover and use the help of your destiny helpers, you run the risk of struggling and suffering endlessly in life with little or nothing to show for your effort. But as soon as you locate your destiny helper, the journey of your life becomes easier and much more progressive. Such was the case of Saul. Until he came face to face with the Oracle of God; Prophet Samuel, he remained in obscurity, working under his father. But within twenty-four hours of contact with Samuel, he was anointed king of Israel [1 Samuel 9 and 10].

The same is the case with Elisha. He remained a small time farmer in his village until, the Oracle of God, Prophet Elijah cast his mantle upon him and his life changed forever [1 King 19:19-21]. Whatever level you are; in life right now! Maybe you are finding it extremely difficult to move to the next higher level! All you need is to locate your divine helper, your destiny helper. I pray this day that God will lead you to your destiny or divine helper in Jesus' name. Amen!

Prayer: I will be divinely led to my destiny helper!

January 23rd

[ONE YEAR BIBLE PLAN: Exodus 7-8 /Matthew 15:1-20]

Today's Word: 2 Kings 17:10

"They set up for themselves sacred pillars and wooden images on every high hill and under every green tree."

WOODEN IMAGE [HEBREW] 'ASHERAH

'Asherah is the Hebrew word for 'wooden image' as used in the above passage and also in [2 Kings 21:7; 2 Kings 23:6] Strong's Concordance #842: This word is both the name of a Canaanite fertility goddess [Asherah] and the designation of a wooden object representing her. In the Old Testament, the word is rarely used as a proper name [2 Kings 21:7; 2 Kings 23:4; 1 Kings 15:13; 1 Kings 18:19] far more often it is used for a carved image. Asherahs were placed on hills. Frequently, so also were altars and other images: [1 Kings 14:23; 2 Chronicles 31:1; 2 Chronicles 33:19].

The Lord warned His people before they entered the Promised Land that this false religion would ensnare them if they did not banish it from the land [Exodus 34:12-16; Deuteronomy 7:2-6; Deuteronomy 12:3; Deuteronomy 16:21].

Nevertheless, the problem persisted during much of the periods of the Judges and kings: [Judges 3:7; 1 Kings 16:33]. Although, occasional reforms did seek to eliminate these images [2 Kings 18:4; Judges 6:25-30]. The prophets consistently sounded a clarion call to abandon such false worship, for God's judgment was coming [Isaiah 17:8; Isaiah 27:9; Micah 5:14 and Jeremiah 17:2].

Fourth Sunday of the Month of January

[ONE YEAR BIBLE PLAN: Exodus 9-11 /Matt. 15:21-39]

CHURCH AND HOME SUNDAY SCHOOL

How does water baptism prepare us for the baptism in the Holy Spirit?

In water baptism, the Holy Spirit prepares our hearts by cutting away the enmity in us and frees us to love God; so much that we welcome the Presence of the Holy Spirit into our lives. Romans 6:4 *"Therefore we were buried with Him through baptism into death, that just as Christ was raised from the dead by the glory of the Father, even so we also should walk in newness of life."*

ARE WATER BAPTISM AND HOLY SPIRIT BAPTISM CONNECTED TOGETHER?

The Scriptures speaks of water baptism and Holy Spirit baptism with fire as one doctrine. The early Believers who received "circumcision of heart" through water baptism were not questioned about how and in whose name they were baptized. Acts 19:1-7 *"And it happened, while Apollos was at Corinth, that Paul, having passed through the upper regions, came to Ephesus. And finding some disciples he said to them, "Did you receive the Holy Spirit when you believed?" So they said to him, "We have not so much as heard whether there is a Holy Spirit." And he said to them, "Into what then were you baptized?" So they said, "Into John's baptism." Then Paul said, "John indeed baptized with a baptism of repentance, saying to the people that they should believe on Him who would come after him, that is, on Christ Jesus." When they heard this, they were baptized in the name of the Lord Jesus. And when Paul had laid hands on them,* the Holy Spirit came upon them, and they spoke with tongues and prophesied. Now the men were about twelve in all."

DOES WATER BAPTISM ALWAYS PRECEDE THE HOLY SPIRIT BAPTISM?

No. The order that the apostles taught was water baptism first and then baptism of the Holy Spirit. However, God sovereignly baptized some in the Spirit before they had been water baptized. Acts 2:38 *"Then Peter said to them; "Repent, and let every one of you be baptized in the name of Jesus Christ for the remission of sins; and you shall receive the gift of the Holy Spirit."*

Acts 10:44-48 *"While Peter was still speaking these words the Holy Spirit fell upon all those who heard the word. And those of the circumcision who believed were astonished, as many as came with Peter, because the gift of the Holy Spirit had been poured out on the Gentiles also. For they heard them speak with tongues and magnify God. Then Peter answered, "Can anyone forbid water, that these should not be baptized who have received the Holy Spirit just as we have?" And he commanded them to be baptized in the name of the Lord. Then they asked him to stay a few days."*

Sunday School Question

1) How does water baptism prepare us for the baptism in the Holy Spirit?
2) Are water baptism and Holy Spirit baptism connected together?
3) Does water baptism always precede the Holy Spirit baptism?

Memory Verse: Acts 10:48 "And he commanded them to be baptized in the name of the Lord. Then they asked him tostay a few days."

January 25th

[ONE YEAR BIBLE PLAN: Exodus 12-13 /Matthew 16]

Today's Word: Psalm 121:1-8

MY FAMILY AND I ARE PRESERVED OF THE LORD!

Some months ago, a lady came to the Tabernacle of Oracle of God [Our Church] and was miraculously healed by the power of the Holy Spirit of goiter. The following is her testimony read on:

Testifying, she said: *"she was afflicted with the disease as she went to seek help of an herbalist, concerning her marital issues. In the process, the priest insisted on sleeping with her. Which she refused and her rebuttal infuriated the witch doctor, who threatened to deal with her. In fulfillment of his threat, the man astral projected into the woman's bedroom that same night. The man mesmerized her, gave her a magical broom and commanded her to start killing flies and feed on them. And she obeyed accordingly as instructed under a spell. In the process of time, she developed the goiter from the habit of eating flies. This she did for close to a decade before the Lord delivered her."* Sister J. Wilson SC.

The above praise report may amaze you but that is exactly the working of the kingdom of darkness. The devil gives you one thing and takes away ten: Satan takes away your freedom. Those whose past-time is to visit diviners, soothsayers, or practice voodoo, juju etc., to resolve their issues exposes themselves to higher demonic manipulations. That is why, this day I admonish you to please return to God and be save!

Prayer: *Lord! I look up to you this day for preservation!*

January 26th

[ONE YEAR BIBLE PLAN: Exodus 14-15 /Matthew 17]

Today's Word: Galatians 3:9

I DECREE! MY FAITH WILL TAKE ME TO THE TOP!

From scriptures we understand that Abraham was wealthy and healthy [Genesis 13:2]. He however, did not become so by hard work alone or by chance [Hebrews 11:8]. In other words, Abraham became great by faith. He took the faith way to the top. You are a child of Abraham by faith therefore; you also must make it to the top in life, by taking the faith way up. The life you live now must be by faith; for the just shall live by faith [Galatians 2:20]. Faith in God and in His Word gives you fabulous results in all your life's endeavors. Without faith, it is impossible to please God [Hebrews 11:6]; anyone that comes to Him must believe that He supplies divine health, divine provisions, divine promotion and all kinds of rewards etc. From scripture we understand that through faith the elders obtained a good report [Hebrews 11:2]. This means that the elders took the faith way up! Extra-ordinary miracles were done through them because they acted on God's Word. Through faith they achieved greatness [Hebrews 11:33]. You also can equally get your bills paid, get a great job, live in divine health, and begin to live victoriously instead of being a victim; living a laborious life.

You can live a life of good success and all round prosperity everyday of your life as you live your life by the Word of God in Faith! Glory to God! [Galatians 3:7] says they which are of faith are the children of Abraham and the promises of God were made to Abraham and his seeds [Galatians 3:16] and that includes you; so like Abraham, get to the top by taking the pathway of faith up!

January 27th

[ONE YEAR BIBLE PLAN: Exodus 16-18 /Matt. 18:1-20]

Today's Word: Isaiah 60:1-5

I DECREE! I SHALL ARISE AND SHINE!

We recognize that every statement in the Bible could be an advice, an appeal or a command. For example; in [Deuteronomy 30:19] the Lord says, I lay before you blessings and curses, life and death, He says; choose life that you and your seed may live! This is an advice.

In [Isaiah 1:18-19] the Bible says; come now, and let us reason together, He says even though your sins is as scarlet, they shall be as white as snow; He said, If you are willing and obedient, you will eat the good of the land! This is an appeal.

And then in [Mark 16:15] Jesus said; Go ye into the entire world and preach the gospel: that's not an advice, it's not an appeal, it's a command. Go! Is a command! And our text-passage above says arise and shine! And this is a command. God is commanding that beginning from now – you shall arise and you shall shine in the name of Jesus. Amen!

But what does it mean to arise? Arise means move to the next higher level, which is God's definition of breakthrough. But, arise could mean different things to different people depending on the level, they you are. When we talk about promotion we are talking about upward movement. I prophesy this year you shall arise and shine in Jesus' name. Amen!

Prayer: Lord! Let Your grace shine upon me this year 2016 and let me arise and shine in Jesus' name. Amen!

January 28th

[ONE YEAR BIBLE PLAN: Exodus 19-20 /Matt. 18:21-35]

Today's Word: 1 Chronicles 4:9-10

"Now Jabez was more honorable than his brothers, and his mother called his name Jabez, saying, "Because I bore him in pain." And Jabez called on the God of Israel saying, "Oh, that You would bless me indeed, and enlarge my territory, that Your hand would be with me, and that You would keep me from evil, that I may not cause pain!" So God granted him what he requested."

O LORD! SUPERNATURALLY ENLARGE MY COAST!

The circumstances surrounding his birth; led Jabez's mother to name him Jabez meaning sorrow; which accordingly, has his life following a pattern of struggles and frustrations. But Jabez knew better. He bluntly refused to accept that fate. Instead, he cried vehemently unto the God of Israel to change his destiny. And Jabez; a man whose very name meant sorrow became "more honorable than his brethren," [1 Chronicles 4:9]

Saint! Has your life been characterized by struggles and frustration? Does your name reflect the unpleasant circumstances surrounding your birth or has the world given you a name that is synonymous with your situation? Now, begin to rejoice because, the end of your struggles has finally come. As you lift your voice and cry unto Him, the God of Jabez, the same yesterday, today and forever; will enlarge your coast and bless you indeed in Jesus' name. Amen! From today, favor will come your way. So, go out there with a renewed mind; for the world is waiting for you to conquer!

Prayer: God of Jabez! Bless me indeed, and enlarge my coast!

January 29th

[ONE YEAR BIBLE PLAN: Exodus 21-22 /Matthew 19]

Today's Word: 3 John 1:2

I WILL PROSPER ALLROUND AS I REPENT!

One of the purposes of the death, burial, and resurrection of our Lord and Savior Jesus Christ is to get you rich: physically, spiritually in wealth and in health as your soul prospers [3 John 2]. But why are we not blessed? In [Matthew 19:8] Jesus replied, ".....but from the beginning it was not so. And how was it in the beginning? In [Genesis 1:4] God saw that the light was good! In [verse 10] God called the dry land Earth, and the accumulated waters He called Seas. And God saw that this also was good. In [verse 31] God saw everything that He had made, and behold, it was very good (suitable, pleasant).

So, what happened after the beginning? [Matthew 13:25] says but while men slept, his enemy came and sowed tare...! Sleep time, is evil planting time. It is the time of tare-sowing. The devil, our enemy came and sowed the idea of sin to Adam, Satan sow tare in our lives through Adam and Eve in [Genesis 3]. What is the solution? The answer is in [Matthew 15:13] "........Every plant which my heavenly Father didn't plant must be uprooted." So let us start by uprooting sin from our lives! Pray now:

Prayer: Lord Jesus! I ask for forgiveness of all my sins! Wash me clean in Your precious blood! Father I will serve You for the rest of my life. O God have mercy on me and save my soul now! Accept me as Your child this day in Jesus' name. Amen*!*

January 30th

[ONE YEAR BIBLE PLAN: Exodus 23-24 /Matt. 20:1-16]

Today's Word: 1 Chronicles 4:1

"The sons of Judah were Perez, Hezron, Carmi, Hur, and Shobal."

SONS [HEBREW] 'BEN'

'Ben' is the Hebrew word for 'son' or 'sons' as used in our text-verse above and also in [1 Chronicles 7:14; Exodus 12:37; 1 Kings 2:1] Strong's Concordance #1121:

This Hebrew noun 'Ben' is probably related to the Hebrew word 'Banah' which means 'to build' a family [Ruth 4:11]. The ancient Hebrews considered sons "the builders" of the next generation. 'Ben' can either refer to a literal 'son' as in [1 Kings 2:1], or to one's descendants as in [1 Chronicles 7:14].

The word may also pertain to an attribute of an individual, as in 'Ben-Oni', meaning "son of my sorrow" and Benjamin, meaning "son of the right hand" [Genesis 35:18]. In the plural, the Hebrew word for sons can be translated children regardless of the gender, as in the phrase "children of Israel" [Exodus 12:37]. Perhaps, the most significant use of the Hebrew word is for Israel's relationship with God. God Himself declared "Israel is My son. My firstborn" [Exodus 4:22].

Prayer: Thank You Lord for the provision of adoption of son ship by faith in Jesus Christ. Amen!

Thank You Lord for accepting me this day!

Fifth Sunday of the Month of January

[ONE YEAR BIBLE PLAN: Exodus 25-26 /Matt. 20:17-34]

CHURCH AND HOME SUNDAY SCHOOL

If a believer receives the Holy Spirit baptism first, is it still necessary to be water baptized?

Yes. In every instance where God sovereignly baptized believers in the Holy Spirit, they were immediately water baptized. The proof of the removal of the enmity in the heart against God can only be by having the heart circumcised in water baptism. [Acts 10:47-48]

WHAT IS THE DOCTRINE OF THE BAPTISM OF THE HOLY SPIRIT? It is the baptism [immersing, marinating, and dipping] of the believer into the Holy Spirit and an entrance into the realm of supernatural spiritual power. [Acts 1:8]

WHAT IS THE PURPOSE OF THE BAPTISM OF THE HOLY SPIRIT? The purpose of the baptism in the Holy Spirit is to endue [clothe] us with power. [Luke 24:49]

Sunday School Question

1) If a believer receives the holy spirit baptism first, is it still necessary to be water baptized?
2) What is the doctrine of the baptism of the holy spirit?
3) What is the purpose of the baptism of the holy spirit?

Memory Verse: Luke 24:49 "Behold, I send the Promise of My Father upon you; but tarry in the city of Jerusalem until you are endued with power from on high."

February 01st

[ONE YEAR BIBLE PLAN: Exodus 27-28 /Matt. 21:1-22]

Today's Word: Psalm 107:15-16

MY BREAKTHROUGH COMES AS I PRAISE GOD!

No matter how wealthy, healthy, strong, and famous you are; you are useless in jail. And many are in spiritual prison spiritually; but for you, God has broken the gates of brass and cut the bars of iron in sunder. So, I can say your breakthroughs have come. As a result, go ahead praise the Lord! Adore Him! Magnify His holy Name! He is worthy to be praised! For He has released you from prison! Your breakthroughs have come! Your glory will begin to shine now! Adored Him! Lift Him high! Say! Lord You're highly lifted up. You're the Most High! Eternal Rock of Ages, King of Kings! Lord of Lords! I AM that I AM, The Lion of the Tribe of Judah! Almighty God Glory be to Your Holy Name! Accept my worship in Jesus' name! Thank You for last month. Thank You for breakthroughs! Thank You for setting me free! Thank You for bringing me into a new month! Thank You for life, and for joy, thank You for salvation! Thank You for healing and deliverance in Jesus' name. Amen!

FEBRUARY BIRTHDAY PRAYERS!

Lord! I commit those born in the month of February and those celebrating any anniversary this month into Your Hands. February is the 2nd month of the year; so let their blessings and miracles be doubled, let their promotion and anointing be doubled. Give them a new beginning of joy, of success, of divine health, of progress and prosperity, and a closer walk with You Lord. Let it be well with them in Jesus' name!

February 02nd

[ONE YEAR BIBLE PLAN: Exodus 29-30 /Matt. 21:23-46]

Today's Word: Daniel 5:11-12

THE SPIRIT OF EXCELLENCE IS UPON MY LIFE!

The passage above is a testament of the queen of Babylon concerning Daniel when the King seeks someone who is able to explain or decode 'the hand writing on the wall'. Base on this reference, Daniel was assign the task to resolve the problem which eventually led to his promotion to the third most powerful person in the land. [Daniel 5:29].

Saint! You must recognize that in the affairs of men the Omnipotent reigneth. When God releases upon you the spirit of excellence, divine wisdom, knowledge and uncommon comprehension; you excel above your contemporaries. And this gives you the ability to live the supernatural life made available to you as a member of the body of Christ; by Christ death and resurrection. In as much as you are born of the Spirit of God, you become a genius. The level at which you operates and your potential; becomes heavenly; as you become divinely endowed. Daniel said I have understanding by the book. Which book? This book of the Law; the Word of God shall not depart from your mouth. Your potential depends on how much you are equipped with God's Word. A Wordless Christian is worthless Christian. The more you meditate on the Word, the more it permeates your soul and spirit for the expression of the God in you. I pray this day that you begin to manifest greatness by the Spirit of the God in Jesus' name. Amen!

Prayer: I receive the endowment of the spirit of excellence!

February 03rd

[ONE YEAR BIBLE PLAN: Exodus 31-33 /Matt. 22:1-22]

Today's Word: Exodus 14:10-30

MY PHARAOH IS SET UP FOR DESTRUCTION!

I can imagine what was going on in the minds of the Israelites during Moses' earlier encounters with Pharaoh. Moses had just returned from the wilderness of Median after forty years with the news that God sent him to deliver them from slavery in Egypt. With great hope, they wait for him to come from Pharaoh with the news of freedom. Instead, Pharaoh retorted, "And said; "Who is the Lord? That I should obey His voice to let Israel go? I do not know the Lord, nor will I let Israel go."

In addition, he punished them by increasing their toil. What an irony! How disappointed and discouraged the Israelite must have felt. But God's ways are different from our ways. While they feared; they never knew that God was setting Pharaoh up for total destruction. Accordingly, from that day, God gradually tortured Pharaoh until his final demise at the Red Sea.

Saint! Maybe the enemy is contesting the deliverance God has promised you a while ago. Maybe God has released your miracle a long time in the realm of the spirit but, the Pharaoh of your life has refused to allow the physical manifestation in this realm. I decree by the decree of heaven the Lord God is setting your Pharaoh up for destruction in Jesus' name. Amen! I decree that the setback you are experiencing now is a setup for your comeback in the name of Jesus Christ. Amen!

Prayer: Lord set my Pharaoh up for total destruction!

February 04th

[ONE YEAR BIBLE PLAN: Exodus 34-35 /Matt. 22:23-46]

Today's Word: Genesis 13:14-18

I DECREE! AN END TO ALL NEGATIVE RELATIONSHIP IN MY LIFE!

There are relationships that cover people's destinies and inherently slow their progress. Until you discover and separate yourself from such associations, you run the risk of becoming unsuccessful and obscure in life. Lot's relationship with Abraham was one of such debilitating associations. For the length of time that Abraham had Lot around; there was little or no progress. According to scriptures, his vision and communication with God were impaired and hindered. But because he was God's friend, a spiritual demarcation was brought between him and Lot. Immediately after their separation, God re-established communication with Abraham and progress began again for Abraham.

Are you in any inhibiting relationship? The relationship may even look good physically but spiritually, it may be a hindrance to your advancement in life. You need to spiritually discern and then severe yourself from all such association; for any meaningful progress to begin in your endeavors. They could be family members as in the case of Abraham, they could be career peers; and even in the church; you find such people everywhere. I tell you the truth; such association must end before delays and stagnancy would end in your life. Saint! You have prayed enough, it is time to take action and free yourself of that extra luggage and baggage in your life!

Prayer: I decree an end to every evil association in my life!

February 05th

[ONE YEAR BIBLE PLAN: Exodus 36-38 /Matt. 23:1-22]

Today's Word: 1 Kings 18:20-30

MY ENEMIES SHALL LOSE THEIR POWER BASE!

The day, the Idol god, Baal was judged by the creator of all things, the prophets of Baal must have been disappointed before they were killed by Elijah. Series of events that lead to the killing of the prophets of God by Jezebel and her husband, King Ahab instituting Baal as the state religion of Israel must have given them the conviction that Baal is indeed the most powerful god in the universe.

The fact that they accepted Elijah's challenge was because they were deceived by illusory manifestation of Baal's gains; but, their source of power was switched off and they all died.

Many a times, unbelievers brag about their evil acts against Believers. They do so by illusory signs and magic that the devil exhibit through them. Most regrettably, many Saints get scared of these threats out of sheer ignorance. I tell you the truth beloved, at the name of Jesus Christ, every knee must bow. When the power of darkness and wickedness encounters the power of the Almighty God, the devil submits completely. So, as believers, redeemed by the blood of Jesus; no power in the entire universe can subdue you.

Do you have enemies threatening you with witchcraft, wizardry and cultic powers? I prophesy your enemy's source of strength shall fail in Jesus' name. Amen!

Prayer: Evil powers congregating against me be scattered by fire in Jesus' mighty name. Amen!

February 06th

[ONE YEAR BIBLE PLAN: Exodus 39-40 /Matt. 23:23-39]

WORD SWORD OF THE ORACLE

Today's Word: 1 Chronicles 5:7

"And his brethren by their families, when the genealogy of their generations was registered: the chief, Jeiel, and Zechariah."

GENERATIONS [HEBREW] 'TOLEDOTH'

'Toledoth' is the Hebrew word for 'generation' as used in the above scripture and also in [Genesis 10:1; Ruth 4:18] Strong's Concordance #8435: This Hebrew word is derived from the verb 'Yalad', meaning 'to give birth.' Toledoth usually introduces an extended genealogical list, such as those in the book of Genesis [Genesis 5:1; Genesis 10:1] and the book of [1 Chronicles 5:7; 1 Chronicles 26:31]. Ancient Hebrew culture depended on detailed genealogical lists to determine questions of inheritance and land use rights.

After the conquest of Canaan, each tribe received its portion of the Promised Land to divide between its clans in [Joshua chapters 13-19.] Land rights remained in the clans, passed down as part of the inheritance from father to the oldest son, or daughter if there was no son [Numbers 27].

Other matters, such as service in the temple and royal succession, were also determined by genealogy. Old Testament genealogies attest to God's faithfulness in fulfilling His promises to make Israel a 'great nation' [Genesis 12:1-3], and the genealogy of Matthew Chapter number 1, shows Jesus as the legitimate heir to David's throne. Glory to God! Alleluia!

First Sunday of the Month of February

[ONE YEAR BIBLE PLAN: Leviticus 1-3 /Matthew 24:1-28]

CHURCH AND HOME SUNDAY SCHOOL

Why is the power [of the Holy Spirit] given to us?

The power of the Holy Spirit is given to us to seal us: Ephesians 1:13 *"In Him you also trusted, after you heard the word of truth, the gospel of your salvation; in whom also, having believed, you were sealed with the Holy Spirit of promise."*

And to give us understanding; to make us effective witness for Christ: Acts 4:33 *"And with great power the apostles gave witness to the resurrection of the Lord Jesus. And great grace was upon them all."* [See also Acts 1:8].

WHAT IS A WITNESS? A witness is one who tells and shows others what Christ has done for him or her. John 3:11 *"Most assuredly, I say to you, we speak what we know and testify what we have seen, and you do not receive our witness."*

Acts 4:20 *"For we cannot but speak the things which we have seen and heard."* [See also Acts 22:15].

Sunday School Question

1) Why is the power [of the Holy Spirit] given to us?
2) What is a witness?

> **Memory Verse:** Acts 1:8 "But you shall receive power When the Holy Spirit has come upon you; and you shall be witnesses to Me in Jerusalem, and in all Judea and Samaria, and to the end of the earth."

February 08th

[ONE YEAR BIBLE PLAN: Leviticus 4-5 /Matt. 24:29-51]

Today's Word: Luke 1:25

GOD SHALL TAKE AWAY MY REPROACH!

The wife of Zechariah, Elizabeth, must have suffered a lot in the hands of many. Her husband as a high priest; and by virtue of that position, he spoke the mind of God unto the people. Expectantly, he must have prayed for many people and they must have received their miracles including fruit of the womb. Yet, his wife could not conceive. Knowing people for what they are; many must have called her names and mocked her bareness. Her situation was a great paradox! No wonder she was so emotional in [Luke 1:25].

Some people's lives are like that of Elizabeth. The people they brought to Christ have got their own miracles. They are so close to God that people are wondering and asking why their miracles are still elusive. They fast and pray on end, kept prayer vigils, sow sacrificial seed etc. And yet it appears as if they will never get result. Are you one of such people? If so, I pray for you now! The Lord shall take away your reproach in Jesus' name. Amen!

It will only take God; just an instant to turn around your captivity. For Elizabeth, the endless years of tears and waiting, ended in [Luke 1:24]. Afterwards, she became blessed among women. [Proverbs 23:18] says surely there is an end. The end of your despair has come this day; for the Lord has taken away your reproach in Jesus' name. Amen!

Prayer: Every reproach in my life is removed now in Jesus' name. Amen!

February 09th

[ONE YEAR BIBLE PLAN: Leviticus 5-7 /Matthew 25:1-30]

Today's Word: Romans 4:20; Mark 10:46-52

I RECEIVE THE RESULT OF DESPERATE FAITH

Desperate faith is one way to achieving good results. In [Mark 10], Jesus visited Jericho. There is no record that He did any miracle there. Imagine, the Prince of Peace himself was in their midst, yet nothing happened during his stay. On His way out of Jericho, a crowd of complacent people followed him. A blind beggar, on the highway, hearing that Jesus is passing by, activated his faith and cried desperately for His touch. Saint! You are the one to trigger your miracle, not God. As long as you remain in your comfort zone, nothing will happen. Many with lots of problems today; say if only they had lived in the days of Jesus, their problems would have been solved. That is an excuse for their unbelief. If you can't reach out in faith to receive your miracle today, you wouldn't have done so when Jesus was on earth, because Jesus always searched for faith in people, and whenever he found one, He always say to them: 'Your faith has made you whole.' Desperate faith is one that resists all odds and oppositions. Any attempt to quench it, rather increase it. It believes that it must receive God's attention now or never.

Jesus could not help but stand still, taking his attention away from everything else; to honor a blind man who demonstrated desperate faith. Release your faith for your desired change. If you have not yet arrived at the place of desperation; it means you can still continue to manage with things the way they are in your life!

Prayer: My desperate faith shall bear fruit in Jesus' name!

February 10th

[ONE YEAR BIBLE PLAN: Leviticus 8-10/Matt. 25:31-46]

Today's Word: Mark 10:46-52

MY GOD SHALL STANDSTILL TO AID ME SPEEDILY!

"And Jesus stood still, and commanded him to be called" [Mark 10:49]." And that marked the beginning of the end of Bartimeus, blindness. Considering the fact that Jesus of Nazareth had to stand still for him, many would have regarded Bartimeus a lucky man. But, a critical analysis will show that he deserved what he got. Bartimeus, a blind man on hearing so many voices, he asked the people what was going on. Then, he was told that Jesus, the miracle worker had just passed by. Realizing that his miracle had just gone by, but determined not to let go, Bartimeus started calling on Jesus with a loud voice. Then, many among the crowd jeered at him and admonished him to be quiet. But that did not deter him [Mark 10:48]. Eventually, touched by his desperation, Jesus stood still and healed him. Alleluia!

Are you in a desperate situation right now? Has Life treated you so shabbily that you are contemplating suicide? Or like Bartimeus, has your miracle passed you by at your unguarded moment? Hear now the Word of God, "Today, Jesus will stand still for you." As you key into this prophecy you shall receive your testimony in the name of Jesus. Amen! Now stand up and call on the name of Jesus desperately, and present your problem to Him. I tell you, this is your season. Jesus will surely give you your miracle today! Alleluia!

Prayer: Lord! Be Merciful and deliver me and my loved ones!

February 11th

[ONE YEAR BIBLE PLAN: Leviticus 11-12 /Matt. 26:1-25]

Today's Word: Hebrews 9:22

MY AFFLICTIONS ARE DESTROYED!

Read this praise report it will surely edify you:

"*Five years ago my 12 yrs old daughter was afflicted by a viral infection. The ailment which manifest as itches all over her body caused her so much discomfort and pain that she could hardly sit still or lay down. Her sleep was restless! I took her for all kinds of test; all kinds of medication were administered without result. I prayed and prayed to no avail. I even prayed that God should transfer the ailment from my daughter to me; but nothing happen! There was no change; matter of fact her condition grow worst. Fortunately, a friend of mine invited me to the Oracle of God revival in Indian Head, MD and it was the last day and we part took in the Holy Communion. In the course of the service Pastor Stevie said I decree by the decree of heaven that any one that is sick here would be healed as they partook in the Holy Communion! Lo and Behold the next day, all the symptoms were gone. Glory to God!* Sister Jane. Delaware.

Saint! Is there an ailment in your life that has defied modern medicine? Is there any demonic deposit in you? Are you afflicted? Is it an infirmity? I decree by the decree of heaven that infirmity and affliction in your life is hereby destroyed in the mighty name of Jesus. Amen!

Prayer: Lord! Destroy by Your fire, every affliction in my life in the name of Jesus. Amen!

February 12th

[ONE YEAR BIBLE PLAN: Leviticus 13 /Matt. 26:26-50]

Today's Word: Galatians 5:6

MY FAITH WILL WORK BY LOVE!

Faith is the principle by which everything works in God's Kingdom. For the just shall live by faith! This tells us how important faith is and why the "Faith-massage" should always be taken seriously by anyone who desires to live a victorious life in the Kingdom of God! Interestingly, however, people walk by faith daily all over the world. Or how else would men have gone to the moon or build a skyscraper if not by faith. But not all faith is the God-kind of faith. God-kind of faith is the faith which works by love; by the love of God. God is love and faith that works by love recognizes God in all things seen and unseen. The faith that works by love is a saving faith, a victorious faith that comes of the amazing grace of God that is imparted unto you by the Word of God.

In this day and age, where there is so much evil and wickedness of the wicked, operating at this realm of faith is required to live a successful Christian live. If your faith works by love, you won't steal or lie or kill to meet your needs. You'd find yourself walking, loving and living peaceably among all men as God instructs us to. You'd even be able to listen and not respond in bitterness when someone speaks evil to you or about you. You remain unruffled and still love them. By faith you'd hold your head up and not allow what your critics' say, make you react negatively, and you won't wish evil for those who hate, malign and mistreat you!

Prayer: Lord! Let my faith work by your love!

February 13th

[ONE YEAR BIBLE PLAN: Leviticus 14 /Matt. 26:51-75]

WORD SWORD OF THE ORACLE

Today's Word: 1 Chronicles 12:18

---

*"Then the Spirit came upon Amasai, chief of the captains, and he said: "We are yours, O David; we are on your side, O son of Jesse! Peace, peace to you, and **peace** to your helpers! For your God helps you." So David received them, and made them captains of the troop."*

PEACE [HEBREW] 'SHALOM'

The Hebrew word for 'peace' is 'Shalom' as used in our text-verse above and also as in [Genesis 43:23; Numbers 6:26; Isaiah 54:13] Strong's Concordance #7965. This word conveys the idea of completeness and well-being: of being perfectly whole. The word denotes an absence of discomfort, whether physical ailments or strife, internal or external [Genesis 43:28; Isaiah 26:3; Ecclesiastes 3:8].

It is used as an ordinary greeting, as a word of assurance, and as a term of blessing [Genesis 43:23; 1 Samuel 25:5-6; 2 Kings 5:19]. The prophets Jeremiah and Ezekiel spoke out against the false prophets of their day for erroneously prophesying peace where there is none coming. [Jeremiah 6:14; Jeremiah 8:11; Ezekiel 13:10; and Ezekiel 13:16] After God's judgment fell, Jeremiah proclaimed that God's thoughts towards the captives were for peace and not evil [Jeremiah 29:11]. The word also occurs in two important messianic prophecies identifying the Messiah as the Prince of Peace and the One who would assure our peace [Isaiah 9:6; Isaiah 53:5].

Second Sunday of the Month of February

[ONE YEAR BIBLE PLAN: Leviticus 15-16 /Matt. 27:1-26]

CHURCH AND HOME SUNDAY SCHOOL

Is the baptism of the Holy Spirit for everyone?

Yes! Acts 2:17 *"And it shall come to pass in the last days, says God, that I will pour out of My Spirit on all flesh; Your sons and your daughters shall prophesy, your young men shall see visions, your old men shall dream dreams."* [See Acts 2:39]

DO WE HAVE THE HOLY SPIRIT WITH US BEFORE WE RECEIVE THE BAPTISM OF THE HOLY SPIRIT?

Yes! The Holy Spirit is the one who draws us to Jesus and reveals His identity to us. *"No one can come to Me unless the Father who sent Me draws him; and I will raise him up at the last day."* John 6:44 The Holy Spirit convicts us of sin and guides us into all truth. The baptism of the Holy Spirit is a gift for Believers to empower them for service and make us effective witnesses of God's grace. John 16:8 *"And when He has come, He will convict the world of sin, and of righteousness, and of judgment:"* [See also Matthew 16:17]

<u>Sunday School Question.</u>

1) Is the baptism of the Holy Spirit for everyone?
2) Do we have the Holy Spirit with us before we receive the baptism of the Holy Spirit?

> **Memory Verse:** Acts 2:39 "For the promise is to you and to your children, and to all who are afar off, as many as the Lord our God will call."

February 15th

[ONE YEAR BIBLE PLAN: Lev. 17-18 /Matt. 27:27-50]

Today's Word: 1 Thessalonians 5:18

"in everything give thanks; for this is the will of God in Christ Jesus for you."

I RECEIVE DIVINE ENABLEMENT TO PRAISE GOD!

It takes strong faith to have an attitude of gratitude. We understand from scriptures that without faith no one can please God [Hebrews 11:6]. So, if giving thanks to God pleases Him, it means thanksgiving amidst trails and tribulation is an attribute or evidence of faith. And God will always reward your faith exhibited in gratitude by doing more than you can imagine. He will do exceedingly; abundantly above your expectation, above what you may ask or can ask. If you believe; why not declare you faith now by appreciating and praising God now!

PRAYER OF THANKS

Father! Glory be to Your holy name. Thank You for peace in our time, thank You because I know my tomorrow will be alright, thank You for everything. Thank You for the youth, thank You Lord for the children, thank You for life, thank You for the Body of Christ, thank You for Your Church. Father, in Your own wonderful way; change my failure to success, change my shame to fame. Father, this month, in my life, show Your glory. Arise Oh Lord! Fight for Your Church, fight for Your Children, fight all my enemies, wherever they may be, Lord uproot them all in Jesus' gracious name. Amen! Thank You for everything Lord, visit me and my loved ones today, save soul, heal the sick, set the captives free and just let Your name be glorified, in Jesus' name I have prayed. Amen!

February 16th

[ONE YEAR BIBLE PLAN: Leviticus 19-20/Matt. 27:51-66]

Today's Word: Luke 4:40-44

I WILL NOT BE LIMITED TO LIFE'S COMFORT ZONE!

When people start experiencing success in lives, there is the tendency to stop aspiring further. This is usually the case when some level of positive result begins to attend to people's effort. Many remain at this level of achievement because of what is called 'comfort zone syndrome.' This syndrome makes many achieve little in life at the end of their youthful years. I pray that you will not be limited to the 'comfort zone' of life in Jesus' name. Amen! Jesus also faced the temptation of being limited by this syndrome in His lifetime. Based on the remarkable result that attended to His ministration in the city of Capernaum, the people began to plead with Him to stay. By their plea, they sought to deitify Him and in their ignorance, ultimately limiting His ministry to Capernaum. But even though Jesus Christ loved the attention He got from His people, He knew that His ministry was to the whole world and should not be limited to one city. That is why He left the 'comfort zone' and extended His frontiers.

Have you discovered your purpose in life? Are you committed to fulfilling it? Know that good things of life can limit you. If you are earning a lot and still remained unfulfilled in your job that is a sign that you're being limited. You must pray and search for the vocation that will give you fulfillment. It is only by getting involved in that which you love; that you can achieve what God planned for you. I pray you won't be limited to a comfort zone in Jesus' name. Amen!

February 17th

[ONE YEAR BIBLE PLAN: Leviticus 21-22/Matthew 28]

Today's Word: Genesis 8:22 & John 3:16

I DECREE! MY HARVEST IS GUARANTEED!

In John 3:16, God set an example for humanity on the law of sowing and reaping. In order to redeem and reconcile billions of children to Himself; He sowed His only begotten son, Jesus Christ. So, God is a sower. He wants us to emulate Him. The law of sowing and reaping is an eternal truth. It is simply accurate and does not fail or delay. God is no respecter of persons. He respects His principles. Since He set the rule in [Genesis 8:22]. The rule is still binding on all of creation today and forever.

Even though, God promised to prosper me abundantly when He called me to ministry, I remained virtually poor after many years of ministrations, yet I could barely survive. Then, one day, I ask the Lord in earnest prayer; why I could not step into the promise for so long. God referred me to the scripture above. On realizing my error, I began to sow heavily into the kingdom, and on men and women of God and then the Lord God began to bless me mightily; instantly, my income recorded a correspondent increase. Saint! I admonish you now to increase your investment in the kingdom of God. It does not matter which ministry you are in. Just find a way of supporting God's work with your substance, your time, your gifts and talents. And as you do so, your harvest is guaranteed in Jesus' name. Amen! Visit: WWW.OOGOD.ORG/ to sow!

Prayer: En-grace me to sow abundantly in Jesus' name!

February 18th

[ONE YEAR BIBLE PLAN: Leviticus 23-24/Mark 1:1-22]

Today's Word: 2 Chronicles 2:6-12

I DECREE! ALL ROUND PROSPERITY UPON MY LIFE!

Has it being difficult to experience all round blessings in your endeavors? Have you been struggling to survive in spite of your intellects, gifts, talents and hard work? Does too much effort produced too little or no result for you? If the above statement describes you in any way; there are two questions you need to answer sincerely now. What is your motive for desiring the blessings you desire? And have you ordered your priorities right? As soon as you answer these questions honestly and make necessary mends, you will observe an outpouring of God's blessings upon your life. Alleluia!

God's ultimate aim is to reconcile humanity with Him [divinity] and ameliorate the problems of mankind. To fulfill that purpose, He is searching out those whose desires and motives are in line with His vision. As soon as He proves such people, He releases blessings upon them to enable them function effectively. That is the key that opened the vault of heaven for Solomon. God Himself made allusion to that when He told Solomon that He was going to bless him abundantly because of his desire to use the blessings to serve the people. What is your disposition towards wealth? Do you hoard the resources God has given you? Do you cheat other people and take away their belongings? Do you embezzle public fund? If so, you need to change for change to happen in your life! And as you do so, you will begin to enjoy all round prosperity in Jesus' name. Amen! Visit: WWW.OOGOD.ORG/ for more!

February 19th

[ONE YEAR BIBLE PLAN: Leviticus 25 /Mark 1:23-45]

Today's Word: 2 Kings 2:1-15

I AM DIVINELY ELEVATED TO A HIGHER HEIGHT!

At various instances on his journey with Elijah from Gilgal through Bethel and Jericho to Jordan, the other sons of the prophets ridiculed Elisha's diligence. But determined to get a double portion anointing upon the life of Elijah, Elisha put up with the insults and persevered. However, when the double portion anointing of the spirit finally rested upon him, the same sons of the prophets "...Came and bowed down to him." [2 Kings 2:15]. The Lord God of Elijah gave Elisha results that removed the insult that was in his life. I pray that the same God of Elijah and Elisha shall give you results that will remove insults from your life in the name of Jesus. Amen!

Maybe people have ridiculed you because of your total commitment to Jesus Christ. Maybe you've been forsaken by the world because of one reproach or the other. People might even be making fun of you because you have nothing to show now for your hard work. Today, I stand as the mouthpiece of the Most High to prophesy that it is your turn to be elevated. The same Spirit that elevated Elisha from obscurity to prominence is hereby released upon you in the name of Jesus. Henceforth as many as have ridiculed you; shall begin to reverence you in Jesus' name. They will surely begin to treat you with utmost respect because the Lord God who changed Elisha's destiny has located you for greatness this day.

Prayer: In agreement with this prophecy, today, I am stepping out of obscurity into prominence in the name of Jesus. Amen!

February 20st

[ONE YEAR BIBLE PLAN: Leviticus 26-27 /Mark 2]

WORD SWORD OF THE ORACLE

Today's Word: 1 Chronicles 13:8

"Then David and all Israel played music before God with all their might, with singing, on harps, on stringed instruments, on tambourines, on cymbals, and with trumpets."

CYMBALS [HEBREW] 'METSELETH'

The word for 'cymbal' in the Hebrew language is 'Metseleth' as use in our text-verse above and also in [1 Chronicles 15:16; 1 Chronicles 16:42; 1 Chronicles 25:6; Nehemiah 12:27] Strong's #4700. The verbal root of this Hebrew word means 'to tingle'; thus the noun form indicates some kind of cymbals, described on one occasion as made of bronze [1 Chronicles 15:19]. Cymbals are always listed with other instruments, and they are regularly associated with singing [1 Chronicles 15:19; 2 Chronicles 5:12-13; Nehemiah 12:27]. On occasions cymbals even accompanied the exercise of prophecy [1 Chronicles 25:1]. David and Nathan established a Levitical order of musicians which includes those who played cymbals, stringed instruments, and harps to glorify God [1 Chronicles 15:16; 2 Chronicles 29:25; Ezra 3:10-11]. The Levitical cymbal player led the musicians in the worship of God [1 Chronicles 16:5]. Cymbals were played during worship and joyful celebrations to the Lord at such times as the dedication of Solomon's temple, Hezekiah's consecration of the house of God, laying of foundation for the second temple, and the dedication of the wall of Jerusalem [2 Chr. 5:11-14; 2 Chr. 29:25-31; Ezra 3:10-11 and Nehemiah 12:27].

Third Sunday of the Month of February

[ONE YEAR BIBLE PLAN: Numbers 1-2 /Mark 3:1-12]

CHURCH AND HOME SUNDAY SCHOOL

What are the blessings of the Holy Spirit baptism?

The blessings of the baptism of the Holy Spirit are:

1. We are enabled to pray in the spirit: [Romans 8:26-27]
2. We are enabled to praise God in Spirit and in truth. John 4:24 *"God is Spirit, and those who worship Him must worship in spirit and truth."* 1 Corinthians 14:15 *"What is the conclusion then? I will pray with the spirit, and I will also pray with the understanding. I will sing with the spirit, and I will also sing with the understanding." [See* Hebrews 2:12].

3. Through our spiritual ears, we can hear the voice of God. [Acts 13:2; Mark 13:11; Acts 1:2].

4. We are made eligible for the gifts of the Spirit and the power of God. 1 Corinthians 14:1 *"Pursue love, and desire spiritual gifts, but especially that you may prophesy."* See also [1 Corinthians 1:5-7; Acts 1:8]

5. We begin to walk in the Spirit, thereby producing the fruits and graces of the Spirit. Galatians 5:25 *"If we live in the Spirit, let us also walk in the Spirit."* [See also Gal. 5:16-23].

Sunday School Question

What are the blessings of the baptism of the Holy Spirit?

> Memory Verse: Galatians 5:25 "If we live in the Spirit, let us also walk in the Spirit."

February 22nd

[ONE YEAR BIBLE PLAN: Numbers 3-4 /Mark 3:13-21]

Today's Word: Lamentations 3:37

I DECREE! EVERY EVIL UTTERANCE AGAINST ME IS NULLIFIED!

In counseling sessions, I have severally come across believers who confessed that their troubles started after someone made evil pronouncement against them. Such situations occur because of ignorance on the part of the believer[s] involved. Such people either are unaware of the power of the spoken Word or the authority of the mouth of believers. Words are spirits; they are both creative and destructive in nature and can manifest within time frames. That is what demonic agents know and take advantage of.

However, according to our text-verse above, Words proceeding from God are much more authoritative and powerful than from any other source. And God's Word is found in the Bible. God does not wish His children evil but good. Therefore, every child of God has power in his or her mouth to cancel any declaration of evil against them and replace it with God's counsel. So, be not afraid because some witches or wizards have made an evil pronouncement over you or because you hear strange voices telling you that you will die. It is God's Word for you that are final. And His counsel is that you shall live and not die. Therefore, I prophesy henceforth, every evil pronouncement over your life is nullified in Jesus' name. Amen!

Prayer: I cancel every evil uttered against me in Jesus' name.

February 23rd

[ONE YEAR BIBLE PLAN: Numbers 5-6 / Mark 3:22-35]

Today's Word: Genesis 13:1-14

I DECREE! THE REMOVAL OF ALL SATANIC VEILS FROM MY EYES!

How does the above passage minister to you? Does it provoke within you questions like; why did God wait until Lot was separated from Abraham before visiting him? Does something in you ask why God used the word 'Now' when He began to speak to Abraham?

Well, I asked such questions until I received spiritual insight into what happened. Unknowingly, Abraham had placed a spiritual blindfold over his own eyes; the moment he took Lot along on his journey: [matter of fact Lot means veil] [Genesis 13:1]. From that very moment he stopped receiving visions from God and his life became stagnant and problematic. But on the day that Lot was separated from, Abraham the blindfold or veil was removed. I decree every spiritual veil and blindfold over your eyes is removed now in Jesus' name!

When you are blindfolded spiritually, you neither locate nor are you located for goodness, for mercy, for miracles and for favor etc. Consequently, you experience stagnation, failures and troubles. There are some factors that causes spiritual blindfold. Some of them are: evil associations, wrong locations, sin, spiritual slumber etc. If you have been blindfolded? You can change your sad story today if you separate yourself from the causes of such blindfolds. And God will deliver you in Jesus' name. Amen!

February 24th

[ONE YEAR BIBLE PLAN: Numbers 7-8 /Mark 4:1-20]

Today's Word: Matthew 4:1-11

I DECREE! MY TRIAL AND TEST SHALL BE THE GATEWAY TO MY TRIUMPH AND TESTIMONY!

Is the way to your breakthrough clustered with hindrances? Are you going through trials or test right now? Beloveth, fear not, for as you focus completely on Jesus Christ your Lord and Savior, you will prevail. Your test will become testimonies, your trials will become triumph, your tribulation and temptation shall become the gateway to your greatness. These obstacles are permitted in your life by God to create your miracles. They are to prove and purify you; and to ascertain your qualification for a greater height. Jesus Christ, the Son of God did not assume His God ordained position until after He had been tempted by Satan the tempter. Jesus had to overcome the obstacle before the miracles started. So also is life with everyone today.

Whether you are a student or not if you desire advancement and promotion in life you must be determined to scale obstacles. You must perform at examinations to get to the next level. Saint! Are you facing one difficulty or the other today? Are you sandwiched and almost submerged in problems? I admonish you this day, confront that situation with the right attitude and your altitude will change for good in Jesus' name. Recognize that at the end of it all; lays a great opportunity for great improvement and advancement in your life's endeavor. Remain Blessed!

Prayer: I receive the grace to overcome the trials of life*!*

February 25th

[ONE YEAR BIBLE PLAN: Numbers 9-11 /Mark 4:21-41]

Today's Word: Colossians 1:23

"if indeed you continue in the faith, grounded and steadfast, and are not moved away from the hope of the gospel which you heard, which was preached to every creature under heaven, of which I, Paul, became a minister."

MY DEEP ROOTED FAITH WILL ANSWER FOR ME!

As a believer, you must be deeply rooted in God's Word of faith. That is how you build prevailing and overcoming faith: the faith that can face any and every challenges of life and win. The scripture typified Abraham as one whose faith was deeply rooted in the Word of God. [Romans 4:19-20]. When your faith is deeply rooted in God's Word, it would be impossible for you to waver! You won't stagger at the promises of God through unbelief. Rather, like Abraham your faith will be strong, and will always prevail. Your confidence in God and his ability grows and make you unshakable, unmovable and eventually untouchable by issues of life. The reason many are not deeply rooted in faith is that; they don't spend quality time studying God's Word.

When you give yourself to careful and diligent study of the Word of God, the Holy Spirit will fill your heart and mind with thoughts of faith that will energize your spirit man with faith exploits. God's Word contains everything you require for success and good life; therefore go for the Word of God! Stay on the Word! If you stick to the Word; speak the Word; do the Word you will become deeply rooted and grounded in faith that can move your mountains and obstacles in life. Glory to God!

February 26th

[ONE YEAR BIBLE PLAN: Numbers 12-14 /Mark 5:1-20]

Today's Word: Philippians 3:12-15

I MUST LEARN FROM MY PAST EXPERIENCE!

Many think Paul's resolve to forget the past and to attain future heights means one's entire past should be forgotten. This is far from the truth. For you to achieve your goal in life, you must learn from your past failures and successes. You must find out why you failed or succeeded; while taking steps to prevent future failures. Daniel was a favored Jewish captive in exile. He remained in the corridors of power and survived several kings and kingdoms. He was able to look in retrospect and trace his past successes to the fear of God, the possession of an excellent spirit, hard work, revelation gifts of the Holy Spirit, prayers and fasting. With these, he retained his strengths and that; guaranteed him greater success for the future. Everyone has a past. Your past may be replete with mistakes and errors. You might have taken several decisions by trial and error that led to certain regrets. You might have kept the company of certain people, even believers, who negatively impacted upon you. If you really desire a favorable end, make amends now where necessary. You may have to cut off that 'proverbial right hand' behind your spiritual instability, or pluck out that 'right eye' which appeared indispensable, to ensure a better future. If you do not learn from the past, you will keep falling over the same stumbling block.

Stop now, and identify those stumbling blocks and then come up with a recipe for removing them. Also, don't allow your past successes to get to your head or else, they will rob you of greater victories. Just glorify God for them!

February 27th

[ONE YEAR BIBLE PLAN: Numbers 15-16 /Mark 5:21-43]

WORD SWORD OF THE ORACLE

Today's Word: 1 Chronicles 16:4

"And he appointed some of the Levites to minister before the ark of the Lord, to commemorate, to thank, and to praise the Lord God of Israel:"

MINISTER [HEBREW] 'SHARAT'

'Sharat' is the Hebrew word for 'minister' as used in the passage above and also in the following scripture: [Numbers 3:31; Psalm 101:6] Strong's Concordance #8334: This Hebrew term can denote honorable, high-level service, either secular or sacred. The secular sense of the term refers to the work of personal attendants, usually those who would succeed the office of the one served [Genesis 39:4; Joshua 1:1; and Joshua 1:5]. The sacred use of the word applies primarily to the work of priests, but occasionally Levites, and at least once for angels [1 Chronicles 15:2; Deuteronomy 17:12; Psalm 103:21 and Hebrews 1:14].

Most of the time the ministering, is described as to or before the Lord, but the Levites are also said to minister to the priest [Numbers 18:2]; to the people [Numbers 16:9; Ezekiel 44:11]; and to the tabernacle [Numbers 1:50]. Ministering before; the Lord occasionally involved music and songs [1 Chronicles 6:31-32 and 1 Chronicles 16:4-5]. Angel also minister to the heirs of salvation [Hebrews 1:14].

Prayer: Lord thank You for making your ministers a flame of fire in the name of Jesus. Amen!

Fourth Sunday of the Month of February

[ONE YEAR BIBLE PLAN: Numbers 17-18/Mark 6:1-29]

CHURCH AND HOME SUNDAY SCHOOL

HOW CAN WE RECEIVE THE BAPTISM IN THE HOLY SPIRIT?

We must obey Christ's command to repent and be baptized. Acts 2:38 *"Then Peter said to them, "Repent, and let every one of you be baptized in the name of Jesus Christ for the remission of sins; and you shall receive the gift of the Holy Spirit."* [See also Acts 5:32]

HOW DO WE RECEIVE THE BAPTISM IN THE HOLY SPIRIT? The Lord God employs two distinct methods of baptism; to baptize believers in the Holy Spirit.

1. By the sovereign act of God. Acts 2:2-4 *"And suddenly there came a sound from heaven, as of a rushing mighty wind, and it filled the whole house where they were sitting. 3 Then there appeared to them divided tongues, as of fire, and one sat upon each of them. And they were all filled with the Holy Spirit and began to speak with other tongues, as the Spirit gave them utterance."* [See also Acts 10:44-48]

2. By laying-on of hands. [Acts 8:14-19]

Sunday School question

1) What must we do to receive the baptism in the Holy Spirit?
2) How do we receive the baptism in the Holy Spirit?

> **Memory Verse:** Acts 5:32 "And we are His witnesses to these things, and so also is the Holy Spirit whom God has given to those who obey Him."

February 29th

[ONE YEAR BIBLE PLAN: Numbers 19-20 /Mark 6:30-56]

Today's Word: 1 Samuel 1:11

THE LORD GOD WILL HONOR MY VOWS WITH ANSWERED PRAYERS

Hannah made a very important vow to the Lord: she said; Lord! Give me a son and I will give him back to you! And her prayers were answered immediately.

Why is Hannah's vow so effective? Her vow was effective because, God needed a prophet in His temple; the High Priest, Eli has gotten old and gone rotten. His children had gone completely away from the Lord. So, God was looking for a prophet and Hannah was looking for a son. And when Hannah said to God, give me a son and You've gotten the prophet You need; it pleased God.

What is the importance of vows in prayers? First of all! You need to know that you can't bribe God. You can't buy precious things like a child from God with money. However, whenever you make a vow, you challenge God. And He will do what you asked for; so as to find out whether you will remember to fulfill your vow or not. In [Genesis 28:20-22] Jacob vowed and said Lord, "If You prospers me, I will build an altar unto You and I will pay my tithes." And God said "All right! I will not just prosper you lightly, I will prosper you exceedingly. In [Genesis 30:43] Jacob became exceedingly great. Make a vow now and pray thus:

Prayer: Lord! I pledge this day I will always vow and pay my vows; please answer me when I call in Jesus' name. Amen!

March 01st

[ONE YEAR BIBLE PLAN: Leviticus 21-22 /Mark 7:1-13]

Today's Word: Daniel 4:28-36 & Joel 2:25-27

GOD WILL RESTORE MY GLORY AS I GLORIFY HIM!

As Nebuchadnezzar began to praise God, and admitted that the Most High ruleth in the affairs of men; not only was his throne restored, he said; excellent majesty was added unto me. As you glorify God today, the Lord God will restore everything you've lost and add excellent majesty unto you and your loved ones in Jesus' name. Why not praise the Almighty God now!

PRAISE GOD

O God as I praise you now restore everything I've lost and add unto me excellent majesty! Father, I bless Your Holy Name, there's none like You! You are the King of kings, and the Lord of lords, You are the Way, the Truth, and the Life, the Alpha, and the Omega, Wonderful, Counselor, Mighty God, the Everlasting Father, the Prince of Peace, the Rock of Ages! Glory be to Your Holy Name in Jesus' name I worship!

MARCH BIRTHDAY PRAYERS!

Father, I commit into Your hand Your children born in the month of March and those celebrating their wedding this month: this is the third month of the year and three is the number of trinity; God the Father, bless them, God the Son prosper them, God the Holy Spirit, grant them triple portion anointing. Triple their blessings and promotion in Jesus' mighty name. Amen!

March 02nd

[ONE YEAR BIBLE PLAN: Numbers 23-25 /Mark 7:14-37]

Today's Word: Isaiah 45:11-12

I DECREE! A GREATER CHANGE FOR THE BETTER IN MY LIFE!

To a large extend, your understanding of the mystery of Christ is what determined how outstanding you become blessed. Most times, as I pray for people, they wonder at the tone, command and choice of words that I use in prayer. In some occasion, I've had to explain my audaciousness to many as to why I command heaven to attend to their needs. In today's word God asks you and I to command Him concerning His creations; this is a demand God placed on us, so I simply comply. And God is faithful, just and duty bound to fulfill your heart's desire if you pray according to His word. Amen!

The reason you are not able to appropriate God's covenant is that you are wanting in righteousness. If you are able to live according to God's standard in obedience, you shall decree a thing and it shall surely come to pass in due season. My calling; as an intercessor, and my determination to provoke the heavenlies by the promises of God's covenant; have resulted in the manifestation of uncommon testimonies of miracles, signs and wonder in the Oracle of God International Ministries. If your life is heading the wrong direction for the longest time; I command the circumstances of your life to turn around in your favor now in Jesus precious name. Amen!

Prayer: I command every area of my life that are stagnant, to experience a turn-around now in Jesus' name. Amen!

March 03rd

[ONE YEAR BIBLE PLAN: Numbers 26-28 /Mark 8]

Today's Word: Habakkuk 3:17-19

I DECREE! I WILL WALK ON HIGH PLACES!

Habakkuk may not be a major prophets of God, but he was a very wise prophet. I'm sure that his work was considered based on the depth of his intellect. In the last three verses of his work, Prophet Habakkuk outlined one of the most potent keys of getting results from God: praising and worshiping Him in spite of the prevailing circumstances and situations.

Many lack the capacity to apply this principle. However, it is an infallible principle that has not failed. From experience I know that it is easy to praise God when all is well. It is easier for people to worship Him when it appears that their prayers are being answered. However, the moment things go the other way; many people would rather pray and complain than praise and worship Him.

That is a selfish attitude that does not allow growth in the kingdom of God. Habakkuk's ability to rejoice in the Lord, even when there was no prosperity and no progress, eventually made God to lift him high. I don't know what you're going through right now, but I do know that there is a high place designated by God for you and you can only get there by praise. I decree as you praise God in your adversity, God will raise you to a high place of prosperity in Jesus' name. Amen!

Prayer: Lord! Give the grace to praise and worship you even in adversity in Jesus' name. Amen!

March 04th

[ONE YEAR BIBLE PLAN: Numbers 29-31 /Mark 9:1-29]

Today's Word: Esther 4:13-14

I DECREE! DELIVERANCE SHALL ARISE FOR ME!

What an emphatic statement of faith! No wonder Mordecai rose from the position of a gate keeper to become a Prime Minister. He was a man of outstanding faith; his declarations in our text-passage above attest to this. It was a time of trouble for the Jews in Shushan. A time when Haman had perfected a scheme to destroy all the Jews in the Persian Empire; he was about to implement the plot to kill all the Jews living in the kingdom.

And this was a period when even Esther, the queen was not willing to stake her life for her people. It was a time when the average Jew had lost all hope of deliverance. But spurred by his faith in God, Mordecai declared that God would deliver His people with or without the queen's help. Consequently, the queen aligned herself with the mission and declared a three day fasting for all the Jews in the land including herself and her aides. And God used her to deliver Israel. Alleluia!

I don't know your situation right now; life may have caged you in a tight spot. I don't care how massive the attack of the enemy seems. But I do know that with God on your side, no mountain of problem is insurmountable in the name of Jesus! And since the Lord God of heaven has sent me to you this day, I decree! Today deliverance is coming for you and your loved ones in the name of Jesus Christ. Amen!

Prayer: O Lord! Arise and deliver me in Jesus' name. Amen*!*

March 05th

[ONE YEAR BIBLE PLAN: Numbers 32-34 /Mark 9:30-50]

WORD SWORD OF THE ORACLE

Today's Word: 1 Chronicles 17:12

"He shall build Me a house, and I will establish his throne forever."

THRONE [HEBREW] 'KISSE'

The Hebrew word for 'throne' is 'Kisse' as used in the above text-verse and also in [Psalm 103:19; Isaiah 66:1]; Strong's Concordance #3678:

The Hebrew word can refer to any kind of seat or chair [Psalm 1:1]; but usually it refers to a seat of honor [Isaiah 22:23]; especially a throne as like in [Esther 5:1]. Frequently, the word is used to denote royal position or authority: [1 Kings 16:11] *"Then it came to pass, when he began to reign, as soon as he was seated on his throne, that he killed all the household of Baasha; he did not leave him one male, neither of his relatives nor of his friends."*

To 'set up' or to 'establish' throne is to establish or confirm, a king and his dynasty. David's throne was particularly important in this respect, for in His Covenant with David, God promised that the throne of David's son would be forever [1 Chronicles 17:12; Psalm 89:4].

Although Solomon and the succeeding kings of Judah sat on David's throne [1 Kings 2:12; Jeremiah 22:2; Jeremiah 22:4] it is Jesus Christ the Messiah, the Son of David, who will fulfill this prophecy, reigning 'upon the throne of David' forever [Isaiah 9:7].

First Sunday of the Month of March

[ONE YEAR BIBLE PLAN: Numbers 35-36/Mark 10:1-31]

CHURCH AND HOME SUNDAY SCHOOL

Do we speak in tongues when we receive the baptism in the Holy Spirit?

Yes! This is initial experience of hearing the Spirit divinely inspired Words and repeating them. 1 Corinthians 2:12-13 *"Now we have received, not the spirit of the world, but the Spirit who is from God, that we might know the things that have been freely given to us by God. These things we also speak, not in words which man's wisdom teaches but which the Holy Spirit teaches, comparing spiritual things with spiritual."*

DOES A PERSON HAVE TO SPEAK IN TONGUES IN ORDER TO BE SAVED? No! Salvation is the work of the indwelling Spirit of God and that has nothing to do with speaking in tongues. The Holy Spirit appeared as tongues of fire on the day of Pentecost to bear witness that the tongue had been sanctified and empowered by God for His use. But speaking in tongues was not necessary for the salvation of these people. Titus 3:5 *".....His mercy He saved us, through the washing of regeneration and renewing of the Holy Spirit."*

Sunday School Questions

1) Do we speak in tongues when we receive the baptism in the Holy Spirit?
2) Does a person have to speak in tongues in order to be saved?

> **Memory Verse:** 1 Corinthians 2:12 "Now we have received, not the spirit of the world, but the Spirit who is from God, that we might know the things that have been freely given to us by God."

March 07th

[ONE YEAR BIBLE PLAN: Deut. 1-3/Mark 10:32-52]

Today's Word: Psalm 106:4-5

THE LORD GOD SHALL REMEMBER ME FOR GOOD!

God never forgets, His capacity to know and remember is beyond human comprehension, there is no searching His understanding. [Isaiah 40:28]. The Lord knows everything about everyone. He knows your end from your beginning; even what you are thinking before you even start thinking; He knows what you are going to think. [Psalm 139:1-6]. God forgets nothing; but He has the prerogative to choose to forget or remember anything; especially your sins.

Whenever God chooses to remember, He moves the heavens and the earth speedily to perform His Word concerning you in remembrance of His promises. Psalms 147:15 says *"He sendeth forth his commandment upon earth: his Word runneth very swiftly."* In [Genesis 41:1-44] when He decided it's time to remember Joseph; within twenty four hours everything changed for Joseph. He became a Prime Minister from being a prisoner. I prophesy everything would change dramatically for you and your family this time as God remembers you in Jesus' name. It does not matter what you are going through right now or how long you've been in that situation. As the Oracle of God I decree by the decree of heaven! The God of Joseph is still on the throne and He will remember you this time for good in the name of Jesus. Amen!

Prayer: Lord! Remember me now for uncommon progress and rapid promotion. Remember my children, remember my marriage! Remember my prayers, fasting, and my alms!

March 08th

[ONE YEAR BIBLE PLAN: Deut. 4-6/Mark 11:1-18]

Today's Word: Daniel 4:28-37

I DECREE! MY LOST GLORY SHALL BE RESTORED!

Sometimes, God in His Sovereign wisdom allows problems in people's life to change certain anomalies in their lives.

Nebuchadnezzar's case was one of such. To correct his perverted perception of his might, God made the king of Babylon to become a beast. In that state, he was now at the mercy of his enemies, and even the elements and was now devoid of whatever glory he had. But, the Bible says surely there is an end to every affliction, especially of the righteous; so at the fullness of time, when he glorified God, his kingdom and glory was restored.

Have you fallen from grace to grass? I tell you saint! There is an end to your affliction. As sure as there is night and day, so also is there a beginning and an end to everything; so today I decree an end to all your afflictions as the Oracle of God in Jesus' name. Amen!

However, the question is; have you learnt any lesson from the adverse situation you are experiencing? For, there is always a lesson or two to learn in every situation. For King Nebuchadnezzar, the lesson was that all power belongs to God, for you perhaps; the same may be the case, or some other lesson or lessons. Whatever it is, learn the lesson, and make amends now. And I decree as you do, your lost glory shall be restored in Jesus' name. Amen!

Prayer: Lord! Restore my lost glory in Jesus' name. Amen*!*

March 09th

[ONE YEAR BIBLE PLAN: Deut. 7-9/Mark 11:19-33]

Today's Word: 2 Kings 3:5-8, 2 Kings 3:21-27

I DECREE! THE CURSE OVER MY LIFE IS BROKEN!

The king of Moab understands the principles of the spirit. After his desperate attempt to flee the offence of Edom, Judah and Israel failed; he realized that his rebellion against Israel has attracted the curse of death upon him and his people. To avert that death sentence, he opted to shed the blood of his eldest son as penance for his rebellion. And since God is a God of principle, He saved the king from death that day.

Many are in all kinds of problem today, because they or their ancestors have rebelled against God, thus incurring the curse of death upon them. Some have been oppressed by generational curses. Many are under constant torment of sickness and diseases because they deviated from God's will. Whatever it is you may be going through; I invoke the power in the sacrificial blood of Jesus, the Lamb of God, and declare every curse in your life; broken now in Jesus' name. Amen!

If God could arise on behalf of Moab, a heathen nation, then He will do much more for you this day! I don't know what you have done to warrant disfavor in your life! I don't know what the legal ground is; that the enemy is using to accuse you before God; that made you fall from grace to grass. But I pray now that the Lord God that spared the king of Moab will spare you in the name of Jesus. Amen!

Prayer: Father Lord! Break every curse operating in my life by the Blood of Jesus. Amen!

March 10th

[ONE YEAR BIBLE PLAN: Deut. 10-12/Mark 12:1-27]

Today's Word: Joshua 6:1-3

THE LORD GOD SHALL GIVE ME A BLUEPRINT FOR SUCCESS!

The secret of the great success of many men and women of exploit can be traced to divine direction. When you are divinely led, you just work from 'the answer to the question' so to say: or in other word, from 'the known to the unknown'. That is what happened in the passage above. As soon as the Lord gave Joshua a blueprint of the outcome of the war he was to undertake, his faith increased because he already knew that he would come out of the war unhurt, alive and victorious.

Having known so, he planned and executed the war [mission] with all the faith and boldness required for success. Do you desire great success like Joshua in your endeavors? Then learn now to seek divine direction. Do you have a project you desire to embark on? Ask God now how to go about it. He is the one that created you. So, He knows what is good for you. He has a blueprint for your success.

More than anything else, as soon as you obtain divine direction or the blueprint of your assignment from God, success is guaranteed in Jesus' name! Do you need the blueprint for great success? Place you right hand upon your head now and declare thus:

Prayer: O Lord God of divine direction! Show me the blueprint for a successful life in Jesus' name. Amen!

March 11th

[ONE YEAR BIBLE PLAN: Deut. 13-15/Mark 12:28-44]

Today's Word: Ephesians 6:16

THE WORD OF GOD SHALL PREVAIL IN MY LIFE!

Whenever you take a bold hold of the Word of God, negative forces rampage and try to steal it from your heart. For Satan knows that without the Word, you are vulnerable to his onslaught. In the parable of the sower; the Word of God said as the sower sowed, some seeds fell by the way side and the birds of the air or evil birds came and picked them. Jesus said these seeds are the Word of God that the hearer did not understand, so the devil comes quickly to snatch it away because it had no root in their hearts. When the Word of God first came audibly and openly to Jesus, in [Matthew 3:17];

Satan tried to undermine it in [Matthew 4:3]. The devil challenged the Word that came to Jesus; however, Jesus wards him off by the shield of faith which is the Word of God [Ephesians 6:16]. He refused to give in to the wiles of the devil by standing on the Word of God, the Word of faith. The devil attacks your faith by throwing darts at you like missiles. He may say for instant; "if indeed you are a new creation repel that pain." You may actually feel sick and weak all over and think you need to lie down. But no! At that point, you ought to use the shield of faith and quench that fiery dart the enemy is throwing at you.

You must get up and shout aloud "I have the life of God in me! Sickness has no place in my body! I walk in strength!" Glory to God! Take a look again at [Ephesians 6:16], in other words the scripture is saying you don't have to cry to God for help to do it; the ability to repel the dart of the devil is already in you so use it! Alleluia!

March 12th

[ONE YEAR BIBLE PLAN: Deut. 16-18/Mark 13:1-20]

WORD SWORD OF THE ORACLE

Today's Word: 1 Chronicles 23:26

*"and also to the **Levites**, "They shall no longer carry the tabernacle, or any of the articles for its service."*

LEVITES [HEBREW] 'LEVI'

This is a brief study on the Hebrew word 'Levi' as in the above text-verse and also in [Numbers 3:9]; Strong's Concordance #3881: The Levites were the descendants of Levi, one of the twelve sons of Jacob. The name is related to the Hebrew verb 'Lavah' meaning 'to join' implying that the Levites were 'joined' to God [Genesis 29:34].

The tribe had three branches, named after the three sons of Levi: the Gershonites, the Kohathites, and the Merarites [Numbers 3]. At Mount Sanai, God chose Aaron, Moses' brother who is a Kohathites to be the nation's high priest [Exodus 28]. No one but the descendants of Aaron could serve as a priest, but the other branches of the Levites shared many of their privileges and responsibilities. Numbers 18:12 *"All the best of the oil, all the best of the new wine and the grain, their first-fruits which they offer to the Lord, I have given them to you."*

Originally the non-priestly Levites helped care for the tabernacle [Numbers 4], but when David began preparations for building the temple, he created new duties for these Levites, making them singers, gatekeepers, treasurers, and royal officials [1 Chronicles 24:1 to 1 Chronicles 26:19].

Second Sunday of the Month of March

[ONE YEAR BIBLE PLAN: Deut. 19-21/Mark 13:21-37]

CHURCH AND HOME SUNDAY SCHOOL

What is the necessity of praying or speaking in tongues?

The Apostles taught that we are strengthened when we pray in the unknown tongue. Our mystical prayers are the intercession of the Holy Spirit to God for us. The neglect of this spiritual exercise produces weak and underdeveloped believers. 1 Corinthians 14:2 *"For he who speaks in a tongue does not speak to men but to God, for no one understands him; however, in the spirit he speaks mysteries."*
See also [1 Corinthians 14:4 [TLB], Romans 8:26-27].

DO WE SPEAK IN TONGUES ONLY AT THE TIME OF OUR BAPTISM? No! We speak in tongues in times of prayer as the Spirit directs us. [1 Corinthians 14:4 (TLB), Romans 8:26-27].

HOW OFTEN SHOULD WE PRAY IN TONGUES? We should pray in tongues in our daily time of devotions, as the Holy Spirit anoints us to. Praying in Tongues edifies, and strengthens us with revelations. [1 Corinthians 14:14, 1 Corinthians 14:18, 1 Corinthians 14:4].

Sunday School Question

1) What is the necessity of praying or speaking in tongues?
2) Do we speak in tongues only at the time of our baptism?
3) How often should we pray in tongues?

Memory Verse: 1 Corinthians 14:4 "He who speaks in tongues edifies himself, but he who prophesies edifies the Church."

March 14th

[ONE YEAR BIBLE PLAN: Deut. 22-24/Mark 14:1-26]

Today's Word: Isaiah 60:1-3 (GWT)

I SHALL ARISE AND SHINE AS I OBEY GOD!

You can surely shine in several things and several ways; you can shine in Gratitude, you can shine in Prayer, you can shine in Anointing, you can shine in Purity, and you can also shine in Obedience. The areas where you shine is usually where others have problems; stars shines at night, because darkness covers the earth, people can see them shine. No darkness; no shining star. No obstacles no miracles!

Many people don't obey God, so you can easily shine in obedience. Your obedience can mark you out from others. Occasionally, God may ask you to do something that may appear foolish, but if you obey Him completely, He will cause you to shine. In Joshua 6:1-20, God said to Joshua, tell the people to go round the wall of Jericho once for seven days and on the seventh day, tell them to go round the walled Jericho seven times, throughout the period don't say a word but on the seventh time, on the seventh day tell them to shout. What! Soldiers marching round a wall like dumb people? Is that the way to fight a war? But they obeyed and won!

Are you trying hard to shine in the midst of darkness? Fear not! But just obey and your yoke will be broken; your light will break forth and you will begin to shine in Jesus' name. Amen!

Prayer: Lord! Let me begin to shine in every facet of life as I obey Your Word in Jesus' name. Amen!

March 15th

[ONE YEAR BIBLE PLAN: Deut. 25-27/Mark 14:27-53]

Today's Word: Genesis 27:1-4 and Genesis 27:25-29

I DECREE! PEOPLE WILL SERVE ME WILLINGLY!

Have you ever wondered why Isaac asked Esau, his son, to prepare meal for him before he blesses him [Esau]? Have you ask why he did not bless Esau right away? The reason is that; Isaac was trying to provoke the anointing of God upon his son so that the blessing will work perfectly and irreversibly.

As a patriarch and a prophet, Isaac understood the principles of the anointing. He understood that the anointing could be provoked by fulfilling a need for God or His prophet. He also knew that the degree of activation of the anointing was directly proportional to the quality of the need met. That is why he asked Esau to prepare a very sumptuous meal for him. That is also why great blessing followed Jacob as soon as Isaac pronounced the blessings; having been satiated.

The anointing of God can be provoked and activated in your life by sowing into the lives of God's servants. The seemingly simple key that Isaac sought to use to bless Esau is also the key that Jacob used to secure the blessing [though fraudulently obtained, it still worked for him]. The Shunamite woman in [2 Kings 4:8-37] used this same key to break the yoke of bareness in her life at old age. You too, can apply this key in your life to receive divine favor. Do you want divine favor? Sow in the life of a servant of God and as you do; I prophesy God's anointing upon you will cause people to serve you in Jesus' name. Amen!

March 16th

[ONE YEAR BIBLE PLAN: Deut. 28-29/Mark 14:54-72]

Today's Word: Matthew 3:13-17

THE GOD OF HEAVEN SHALL APPROVE OF ME!

From numerous prophecies that signaled His coming, unto His manner of birth; death; burial and resurrection; it was clear that Jesus Christ was the only begotten Son of God. When He was yet a little boy, closed members of His earthly family knew that He was a divine child.

But, do you know that Jesus Christ didn't perform anything spectacular until divine approval came upon Him? Do you realize that He did not perform any miracle until He was audibly announced by God from heaven? Do you know that though; He, being the Son of God; anointed from birth; it was only after His baptism and consequent approval that the Spirit of God led Him to fast for forty days in the wilderness? [Matthew 3:17].

Maybe your life has been uneventful since you were born. Maybe you have been unable to optimize your potentials thus far. This day, like it was for Jesus! I pray that heaven will approve your success; I decree by the unction of the Spirit; heaven will approve of you in Jesus' name. From now on, life's condition will be more favorable to you. The problems of your life are coming to an abrupt end this season in Jesus' name! Your voice shall be heard globally and generationally too because this day heaven has approve of you for success!

Prayer: Lord as You approve of me, let me begin to bear good fruits in Jesus' name. Amen!

March 17th

[ONE YEAR BIBLE PLAN: Deut. 30-31/Mark 15:1-25]

Today's Word: James 5:16-17 (NKJV)

THE LORD GOD SHALL GRANT ME THE GRACE TO PRAY EFFECTIVELY!

There are certain hindrances to answered prayers. Firstly, Curse: No sin, no curse simple! Proverbs 26:2 (NIV (UK)) says *"Like a fluttering sparrow or a darting swallow, an undeserved curse does not come to rest."* So sin: the transgression of God's law; gives legal ground for curses in our lives and hinders prayers Isaiah 59:1-3.

Secondly, Covenants with other gods: i.e. soliciting and patronizing, witches and wizards, physic, subscribing to horoscope and all sort of evil candle burning, palm reading, card reading, tarot reading, and living your life by zodiac signs etc., are all covenants that hinder prayers.

Let's assume you have broken all curses and covenants by living a righteous life. And your prayer remains unanswered. [James 5:16-17] says your prayers are not effective because you asked amiss. But if you pray effectively without result, your prayers may not be fervent enough or you are not righteous as you claim to be. So, right now I admonish you; confess and repent of your sins and pray the following scripture:

Prayer: Ephesians 6:11 says "Put on the full armor of God so that you can fight against the devil's evil tricks."

Lord Jesus, wear me your full armor in Jesus' name. Amen!

March 18th

[ONE YEAR BIBLE PLAN: Deut. 32-34/Mark 15:26-47]

Today's Word: Psalm 121:8

MY GOING OUT AND COMING IN IS PRESERVED!

In his book "Left for Dead", Dr. K.A. Paul hypothesized that it was impossible for the devil to take the life of any person who is committed to serving God. When you're committed to serving the Lord, you become an untouchable covenant child of God. God did it for Daniel, and the Hebrew trio etc. He still protects His own in this day and age. Read this praise report:

"Last summer, I traveled to NY, to renew my passport at the Nigeria Embassy. Right in the street, suddenly, gunfire erupted: everybody was ducking their heads and a man fell upon me and I fell on the ground. I thought I've been hit; for I felt warm blood soaking my clothes unto my skin. I was conscious but confused; with sirens, and paramedic all around. The next thing I realized was policemen pulling the weight of a dead body of my back and placing him in a body bag. And two or three people saying can you hear me ma'am? Are you okay ma'am? As they took me to an ambulance and found that it was the blood of the man that fell upon me that was all over me. The man took six slugs in my stead. Then I remember what Pastor Stevie said the previous Sunday in the church that God will preserve and protect the life of anyone connected with the Oracle family even with the life of others this season. I just want to thank God confirming His Word in my life! Sister D. Raleigh NC.

Prayer: Lord Jesus! Preserve my going out and coming in Jesus' name. Amen!

March 19st

[ONE YEAR BIBLE PLAN: Joshua 1-3/Mark 16]

Today's Word: 2 Chronicles 6:3

*"Then the king turned around and blessed the whole **assembly** of Israel, while all the assembly of Israel was standing."*

ASSEMBLY [HEBREW] 'QAHAL'

'Assembly' is 'Qahal' in the Hebrew language as used in the above text-verse and in [Deuteronomy 18:16; Judges 20:2] Strong's #6951: This word denotes a gathering of people for any occasion. It is used in a secular sense to designate civil meeting, war counsels, a gathering of evildoers, and even an assembly of the dead [1 Samuel 17:47; 1 Kings 12:3; Psalm 26:5; Proverbs 21:16]. But the word is also used to speak of the gathering of individuals for religious purposes, such as the receiving of the Mosaic Law and the celebration of religious festivals before the Lord. [2 Chronicles 30:23; Deuteronomy 5:22].

Sometimes, the term applies to groups of men only: most frequently with assemblies for war, but once; apparently, for those gathered to hear Joshua's reading of the Law in [Joshua 8:35]. During the time of Ezra, women, children, and even servants were specifically included in one religious assembly [Ezra 2:64-64; Ezra 10:1]. The expression "assembly of the Lord" occurs several times in the Old Testament to indicate a gathering of God's people for religious or secular purposes including once to grumble against Moses [Numbers 20:4; Deuteronomy 23:1-3; 1 Chronicles 28:8 and Nehemiah 13:1].

Third Sunday of the Month of March

[ONE YEAR BIBLE PLAN: Joshua 4-6/Luke 1:1-20]

CHURCH AND HOME SUNDAY SCHOOL

What is the Anointing?

It is the abiding presences of God, the Holy Spirit. 1 John 2:27 *"But the anointing which you have received from Him abides in you, and you do not need that anyone teach you; but as the same anointing teaches you concerning all things, and is true, and is not a lie, and just as it has taught you, you will abide in Him."*

1 John 2:20 *"But you have an anointing from the Holy One, and you know all things."*

IS THERE A SPECIAL [BEYOND THE ORDINARY] ANOINTING OF THE HOLT SPIRIT?

Yes! The special anointing is the presence of the Holy Spirit through which we receive divine aid for some specific task. It can be compared to the physical reaction we experience in times of danger, stress, etc; when the body begins to secrete adrenalin to give additional strength and alertness. The same holds true when we are anointed. We receive that extra surge of spiritual energy when it is needed. Acts 3:6-8; Acts 19:11-12

Sunday School Question

1) What is the anointing?
2) Is there a special [beyond the ordinary] anointing of the Holy Spirit?

> Memory Verse: 1John 2:20 " But you have an anointing Fromthe Holy One, and you know all things."

March 21st

[ONE YEAR BIBLE PLAN: Joshua 7-8/Luke 1:21-38]

Today's Word: Jeremiah 32:27 (Amp)

"Behold, I am the Lord, the God of all flesh; is there anything too hard for me?

MY HEART DESIRE WON'T BE TOO HARD FOR GOD!

The following testimony is edifying: "The hall was filled inside and out; there was a man whose left kidney was removed in a surgery. The day the kidney was removed there were all kinds of complication. But in our revival the great physician, sent His healing Word; and the Word of God came that: *"there is someone here, one of your kidney has been removed and the second one is giving you problem and God says He's giving you two new kidneys."* And the man looked round and said; Wao! So God can just pick me out for healing among this crowd. This was a Saturday night in August 2010, the next Monday he went to his doctor and the doctor examined him and said what am I seeing, I remember the trouble we went through trying to remove one of your kidneys but now there are two new kidneys." Glory to God!

When we talk about total recovery, we are talking about the only One who can make anything possible. In [Genesis 18:9-14], God told Sarah she would have a son. Sarah was already approaching 90 yrs of age and her husband, 100 yrs old. It was forty years ago she had her last menses. She laughed and God said, why are you laughing? Is anything too hard for me? I don't know what you've being waiting for; but I come to declare to you God's counsel; He will surprise you this time.

Prayer: O God! My heart desire will not be too hard for you*!*

March 22nd

[ONE YEAR BIBLE PLAN: Joshua 10-12/ Luke 1:39-56]

Today's Word: Judges 6:13-14

I DECREE! EVERY LONG STANDING ISSUE IN MY LIFE IS OVER WITH!

Ecclesiastes 3:1 says, *"To everything there are seasons and a time to every purpose under heaven."* So, the problem in your life started one day, and it definitely has to end someday. For seven long years the children of Israel cried under the repressive captivity of Median. Then the Lord heard their cries and sent His angel to Gideon saying, *"Go in this thy might and thou shall save Israel from the hand of the Midianites..."* [Judges 6:14] Backed by the anointing of God, Gideon and his army of a mere three [300] hundred men defeated the Median army numbering over one hundred and thirty five thousand fighting men [Judges Chapters 7 & 8].

Have you been crying to God because poverty and lack have held you captive? Are you under the burden of unemployment, years after your graduation? Whatsoever is the cause of your worries today, I come in the name of the LORD of hosts to declare that; that long-standing problem of yours is over now in Jesus' name. Amen!

The Word of God says, *"Surely there is an end and thine expectation shall not be cut off".* As the LORD liveth, you are entering into a new lease of life because the Lord who sent Gideon to liberate Israel has sent me with the same anointing to terminate your time in captivity in Jesus' name. Amen!

Prayer: Every long-standing problem in my life is over now!

March 23rd

[ONE YEAR BIBLE PLAN: Joshua 13-15/Luke 1:57-80]

Today's Word: Daniel 6:1-3

I DECREE! I SHALL BE SINGLED OUT FOR LIFTING!

Saint! Do you seek divine elevation in your endeavors? Do you seek glory, power and authority to be bestowed upon you? Do you desire to be honored and distinguished among men?

Proverbs 4:7 says wisdom is a principle thing; indeed, that is very true. Wisdom is the major component required for outstanding success in life. It is because of wisdom that Daniel; a captive in a foreign land was set above all the other rulers in the kingdom. [Daniel 1:4] says Daniel and his three friends were young men with outstanding, knowledge, intellect, ability and understanding. That was the basis for their first promotion.

In later years, Daniel was elevated because the king discovered an excellent spirit in him. That qualified him for positions that were the exclusive preserve of the Babylonians. I don't know what position you now occupy in life. Maybe you are still lumped up with all the other staff in your workplace. Maybe you are not yet distinguished in your discipline. Today, I release that excellent spirit that was found in Daniel upon you now. And you can do well for yourself if you begin to study hard and seek knowledge much more ferociously. As you do so, you shall be singled out for divine elevation and exaltation in Jesus' name. Amen!

Prayer: I receive the spirit of excellence from God now!

March 24th

[ONE YEAR BIBLE PLAN: Joshua 16-18/Luke 2:1-24]

Today's Word: 1 Kings 22:29-37; 1 Kings 20:26-34

I DECREE! I WONT FALL VICTIM TO UNGREATFUL BEN-HADADS!

As you grow in God's Word, you come to a point where you begin to wonder why God said He chooses whom He would have mercy on. Experience taught me that there are people who do not deserve mercy. Matter of fact, showing mercy to certain people is not only a mistake, but could be extremely dangerous. So we all need wisdom in exercising mercy!

In the text-passages above, King Ahab captured Ben-Hadad, and had the opportunity to destroy him, but he chose to show him mercy at Ahab's detriment. They made a treaty and amnesty ensued; that for his life, Ben-Hadad is to restore unto King Ahab all the cities the predecessors of Ben-Hadad had taken from the people of Israel. Three years later, Ben-Hadad went back on his word or pledge. Enraged by this new development, Ahab went to war against him to recover the lost land. Ben-Hadad the ingrate, instructed his captain that; the death of King Ahab is top priority: proving that he does not deserve mercy at all. What a terrible way to repay a good gesture. Regrettably, very many individuals are made of the same stuff as Ben-Hadad. There are people who hate your progress in your endeavors. Your promotion and advancement is offensive to them. They use your kindness against you. But, I prophesy this day, you will not fall victim of ungrateful elements in Jesus' name. Amen!

Prayer: Lord! Deliver me from the hands of ungrateful people!

March 25th

[ONE YEAR BIBLE PLAN: Joshua 19-21/Luke 2:25-52]

Today's Word: 2 Corinthians 5:7

I DECREE! I WILL WALK BY FAITH AND NOT BY MY SENSES!

Christianity is a walk of faith. So we must walk the walk not just talk the talk. Faith is a lifestyle! In the N. T., especially the Epistles, there's nowhere we're ask to have faith; because we already have faith as Believers: Rom. 12:3. God wouldn't ask us to walk by faith if we didn't already have faith. You can either walk in faith or by your senses. Rom. 9:8 says *"the children of the flesh are those who are ruled by their senses."* Instead of walking by faith, many walk by their sensory perceptions. This means they walk by their senses: by what they see, hear, touch, taste or smell. Man is a spirit that has a soul and lives in the body. 2 Corinthians 5:6 says your body is not you; it is the place of your abode while you're here on earth. We don't behold God face to face every hour; the way people in heaven do. But we know He's with us? He told us He's with us always Matthew 28:20. Therefore, we don't have to wait to feel His presence because whether we feel it or not, He's with us; God is real than more than what we feel.

Many say I don't feel the presence of God anymore. They are moved by their feelings, instead of relying on the Word of God. Don't live your life base on your senses; live by faith. Don't say I have headache, because you feel some discomfort in your head; refuse to accept it; instead say though I feel headache; I refuse to accommodate it, for I'm healed of the Lord!" Amen!

March 26th

[ONE YEAR BIBLE PLAN: Joshua 22-24/Luke 3]

Today's Word: 2 Chronicles 7:14

*"if My people who are called by My name will humble themselves, and **pray** and seek My face, and turn from their wicked ways, then I will hear from heaven, and will forgive their sin and heal their land."*

PRAY [HEBREW] "PALAL"

The Hebrew word 'Palal' means 'to pray' as used in our text-verse [2 Chronicles 7:14] and also in [Genesis 20:7; Numbers 21:7; 1 Kings 8:44; Isaiah 16:12 and Jeremiah 7:16] Strong's #6419: The Hebrew verb translated 'pray' in God's promise concerning the revival of Israel in [2 Chronicles 7:14] can also mean 'to intervene' 'to interpose', 'to arbitrate,' or even 'to judge'. God ask His people to intercede for others in their prayers. During the dedication of the temple, Solomon modeled intercessory prayer in [1 Chronicles 6:3-42]. He pleaded with God on behalf of the people and continued to pray with determination until the Lord answered. According to the Lord, this type of prayer would be the catalyst for revival and restoration in the future. See also [Daniel 9:3-19].

There are at least six kinds of prayer in scripture: [1] The Prayer of Agreement [Matthew 18:19]; [2] The Prayer of Faith [Mark 11:24]; [3] The Prayer of Consecration and Dedication [Luke 22:41-42]; [4] The Prayer of Praise and Worship [Luke 2:20]; [5] The Prayer of Intercession [Ephesians 1:15-18]; [6] The Prayer of Binding and Loosing [Matthew 18:18-19].

Fourth Sunday of the Month of March

[ONE YEAR BIBLE PLAN: Judges 1-3/Luke 4:1-30]

CHURCH AND HOME SUNDAY SCHOOL

How necessary is the anointing?

Without the anointing, we are totally ineffective in our service to God and man. John 15:5 *"I am the vine, you are the branches. He who abides in me, and I in him, bears much fruit; for without Me you can do nothing."*

IS THE ANOINTING NECESSARY FOR SPEAKING IN TONGUES? Yes! When we speak or pray in tongues without the anointing of the Holy Spirit, it is fruitless and completely meaningless. Acts 2:4 *"And they were all filled with the Holy Spirit and began to speak with other tongues, as the Spirit gave them utterance."* See also [1 Corinthians 12:11; John 6:63; 2 Corinthians 3:5-6].

BIBLE NARRATIVE: Nadab and Abihu, the sons of Aaron, were slain by the Lord for using "strange fire" to burn incense before the Lord. This typifies the outcome of the use of carnal means to kindle the fire of devotion. [Leviticus 10:1-4].

HOW DO WE MAINTAIN THE ANOINTING? By continually abiding in Jesus Christ: [John 15:5]

Sunday School Questions

1. How necessary is the anointing?
2. Is the anointing necessary for speaking in tongues?
3. How do we maintain the anointing?

> **Memorize:** John 15:5 "I am the vine, you are the branches. He who abides in me, and I in him, bears much fruit; for without Me you can do nothing."

March 28th

[ONE YEAR BIBLE PLAN: Judges 4-6/Luke 4:31-44]

Today's Word: Jeremiah 30:16-17, Daniel 3:8-30

I DECREE! I AM DELIVERED FROM THE FIERY FURNACE OF LIFE!

King Nebuchadnezzar's fiery furnace was so hot that it could destroy the shackles that were used to bound Shedrach, Meshach and Abednego. It was so scotching that it burnt to death; the men that took the three Hebrews to the fire gate; but it was not hot enough to burn even a strand of the hair of Shedrach, Meshech and Abednego. Awesome miracle!

Saint! I tell you the truth! That is how God is going to deliver you from the fiery furnace of life in the name of Jesus. The furnace of life connotes poverty, lack, sickness, diseases, despair, all kinds of affliction of life and even death. Your enemies might have set you up to lose your freedom and even your life like these Babylonian princes did to Shedrach, Meshach and Abednego. They may have increased the intensity of the pressure like they did with the fire in our text-passage above.

They may have perfected their plans with the belief that there is no escape for you. But I bring you good news from heaven this day; my God shall deliver you from the fiery furnace of life in Jesus' name. Amen! Just like the Hebrew trio; you are coming out of your present travails unscathed in Jesus' name. Amen!

Prayer: Father! Deliver me from the fiery furnace of life in the name of Jesus. Amen!

March 29st

[ONE YEAR BIBLE PLAN: Judges 7-8/Luke 5:1-16]

Today's Word: 1 Kings 18:43-45

I SHALL DISCERN MY MIRACLE AFAR THIS YEAR!

Imagine a cloud the size of a hand. What kind of rain do you think such a cloud can bring down? Perhaps a drizzle if any; but it was not so. That small cloud that was the size of a man's hand heralded a very heavy rain that consequently, ushered in a new realm of prosperity in the Land of Israel after three long years of drought and economy depression. It took the spirit of discernment for the Oracle of God, Prophet Elijah to know that the insignificant cloud would bring forth mighty rains. If you must make remarkable progress, you must be able to discern when a breakthrough is about to come your way. Most times breakthrough come disguised as problems. Severally, many people have come to me for prayers and counseling for increased incomes. Not long after the prayers, some of them lose their jobs. And after a while, they get greater and better paying jobs and position. Sometime God 'stops the flow to begin the overflow' in your life. God sometimes closes 'one small door to open a bigger and better door or doors' for you.

You need to be sensitive in the spirit to discern whether a difficult situation is a blessing in disguise. I don't know what you are going through right now in your life. But, I can tell you assuredly, that there is a blessing in every storm of life. But you need a closer walk with God to stand the storm. When you do so, God will give you the required spiritual sensitivity to recognize your coming breakthrough. I decree! You shall discern your miracle afar in Jesus' name. Amen!

March 30th

[ONE YEAR BIBLE PLAN: Judges 9-10/Luke 5:17-39]

Today's Word: Joshua 6:1-20

I DECREE! EVERY SPIRITUAL BARRICADE SURROUNDING MY BLESSINGS IS DESTROYED!

By giving Joshua the formula for the fall of the wall of Jericho, the Lord symbolically revealed to us the key to destroy spiritual barricades of the devil. By asking Joshua to make the Israelites go round the wall of Jericho in a certain order for seven days, He was simply letting us know the secrets surrounding demonic enclaves.

Each time we pray against identified spiritual obstacles, the problem is surrounded by a ring of anointing. As we keep up the prayer, fasting and vigils etc., the anointing continues to increase until the restive forces of darkness are finally dissolved. It is at that instant that the barricade is destroyed and testimonies are recorded. Have you been trying unsuccessfully to make progress in life? Have you been finding it difficult to enjoy the blessings that God has released upon you? If so, there is a spiritual barricade surrounding your blessings. And no matter how difficult the situation is; there is a solution in Christ Jesus!

Persistence prayers in His name will bring down that barricade to your breakthrough. No matter how tough your barrier is, it can't be as impregnable as the wall of Jericho. And if the wall of Jericho could come down by God's power; then the barrier surrounding your blessing is coming down this day in the name of Jesus' name. Amen!

March 31st

[ONE YEAR BIBLE PLAN: Judges 11-12/Luke 6:1-26]

Today's Word: Psalm 66:17-119 (CEV)

AS I DISCARD SIN; GOD WILL HIGHLY REGARD ME!

Repentance is one of the keys to attracting God's attention. Christianity is not a religion. Christianity is a fellowship of relationship. There are natural or normal relationships like husband and wife relationships, parents and children relationships. We also have human and animal relationship. There are also abnormal and sinful relationships of Gay, homosexualism and lesbianism etc. We also have relationship with God and our fellow Christians. Your relationship with God must be uncommon or extraordinary to draw God's attention to you for breakthrough in all aspect of your life. Isaiah 59:1-2 (CEV) says *"The LORD hasn't lost his powerful strength; he can still hear and answer prayers. Your sins are the roadblock between you and your God. That's why he doesn't answer your prayers or let you see his face."* The first step to establishing a good relationship with God; is to confess and repent of your sins and ask for forgiveness. And then forgive others of their trespasses against you.

NOW REPENT BY PRAYING THUS!

Father, I believe in Your Son Jesus Christ, I confess to You all of the wrong and sinful things that I have ever done. I ask that You forgive me and wash away all my sins by the blood that You personally shed for me on the cross. I accept You as my Lord and Savior. I ask that You come into my life and live with me for all of eternity. I believe that I'm truly saved and born again now in Jesus' name. Amen!

April 01st

[ONE YEAR BIBLE PLAN: Judges 13-15/Luke 6:27-49]

Today's Word: Psalm 8:2

I DECLARE! GOD'S ORDAINED PRAISE UPON ME!

God has ordained strength, or 'perfect praise', out of the lips of kids. Praise is "strength." To praise is to eulogize God. There is only One 'Holy One' who is worthy of our praises; and that is the Almighty God! "Thou art worthy of all praise," says the Psalmist. Praise Him now!

PRAISE EL-SHADDAI NOW!

O God, I give You honor, glory and adoration. I Praise You! I appreciate You. I magnify Your Holy name. You are worthy to be adored and honored! You are the king of kings and the Lord of lords, the Ancient of days! The I Am that I Am. You are worthy to be praise, so I praise You in Jesus' name. Amen!

APRIL BIRTHDAY AND WEDDING ANNIVERSARY PRAYER!

Lord, I commit unto Your hand; all Your children born in the month of April and those celebrating any anniversaries this month. Number four; is the number of balance; Lord balance everything that is imbalance in their lives! From the East and the West; send them divine helper; from North and South send them destiny helpers. In their homes, let there be peace, harmony, and joy, let there be progress, give them a brand new beginning; of success, of progress, of miracles, of testimonies in Jesus' gracious name. Amen!

April 02nd

[ONE YEAR BIBLE PLAN: Judges 16-18/Luke 7:1-30]

WORD SWORD OF THE ORACLE

Today's Word: 2 Chronicles 12:2

---

*"And it happened in the fifth year of King Rehoboam that Shishak king of Egypt came up against Jerusalem, because they had **transgressed** against the Lord."*

TRANSGRESSED [HEBREW] 'MA'AL'

The Hebrew word for 'transgress' is 'Ma'al' as used above in our text-verse and also in [Leviticus 6:2; Ezekiel 14:13] Strong's Concordance #4603: The principle sense of this word is 'to break a trust,' most often willfully but in some cases unintentionally [Leviticus 5:15]. The term is used in association with the word; sin on several occasions [Leviticus 1:15; 2 Chronicles 6:2; Ezekiel 18:22-24].

Transgression is almost always against the Lord and may be committed by individuals or communities, especially the covenant community [Numbers 31:16; Nehemiah 1:6-7; Ezekiel 14:13]. Also spouse can transgress against each other, or a king can transgress by not rendering a true judgment [Numbers 5:12; Proverbs 16:10]. The word occurs predominantly in the exilic and postexilic books. Then, their death, military defeat, and exile are all viewed as divine judgments on the Children of Israel's transgressions [2 Chronicles 12:1-9; 1 Chronicles 10:13; Ezekiel 39:23 and Daniel 9:7].

Prayer: Lord! Wash away my transgression in the blood of Jesus!

First Sunday of the Month of April

[ONE YEAR BIBLE PLAN: Judges 19-21/Luke 7:31-50]

CHURCH AND HOME SUNDAY SCHOOL

How may we receive the baptism in the Holy Spirit?

You may follow the following instructions:

1. You pray to God through the Lord Jesus Christ for forgiveness of sin and cleansing of the soul and spirit, so that you may approach Him with confidence. [Psalm 24:3-5].

2. Pray to God through the Lord Jesus Christ for the gift of the Holy Ghost. Luke 11:13 *"If you then, being evil, know how to give good gifts to your children, how much more will your heavenly Father give the Holy Spirit to those who ask Him!"*

3. Believing that God has heard you prayer; and then enter into praise, thanksgiving and worship through psalm and hymns until an atmosphere is created for the presence of the Spirit of God. Psalm 134:2 *"Lift up your hands in the sanctuary, and bless the Lord."* See also [Psalm 100:4].

4. When we become aware of the presence of the Holy Spirit, there is a breaking within you and your spirit springs up to respond to the Spirit of God. James 4:8 says *"Draw near to God and He will draw near to you."* Cleanse your hands, you sinners; and purify your hearts, you double-minded." Says the Lord! See [Psalm 84:2; Psalm 51:17].

5. While our spirit is melted in the Lord's presence, we surrender ourselves to God. Romans 12:1 *"I beseech you therefore, brethren, by the mercies of God, that you present your bodies a living sacrifice, holy, acceptable to God, which is your reasonable service."*

[An anointed servant of God may lay hand upon you to impart the Holy Spirit on you.] See also [Acts 8:17; Acts 19:6].

6. When the Spirit of God descends upon you, your organs of speech are stimulated producing the stammering of lips which will form into syllables or words as you yield to the prompting of the Holy Spirit. The words will not be understandable to you because they are prompted by the Spirit rather than your mind. Isaiah 28:11 *"For with stammering lips and another tongue He will speak to this people."* See also [1 Corinthians 14:21].

7. As the Spirit of God overwhelms you, your own words are no longer adequate to praise God. The Holy Spirit then leads us, encourages you and prompts you, but does not force you to speak. However, once we begin, the language is spontaneous and fluent. Mark 16:17 *"And these signs will follow those who believe: In My name they will cast out demons; they will speak with new tongues."* See also [1 Corinthians 14:2].

8. And as you yield; you begin to speak in tongues. Acts 2:4 *"And they were all filled with the Holy Spirit and began to speak with other tongues, as the Spirit gave them utterance."* See [2 Peter 1:21].

Sunday School Question

1) How may we receive the baptism in the Holy Spirit?

> **Memorize:** Mark 16:17 "And these signs will follow those who believe: In My name they will cast out demons; they will speak with new tongues."

April 04TH

[ONE YEAR BIBLE PLAN: Ruth 1-4/Luke 8:1-25]

Today's Word: Psalm 30:3-5

I DECREE! THIS IS MY LAST NIGHT OF WEEPING!

This praise report will edify you, read on:

"There was no desired result from all the medication to stem the fibroid condition I am diagnosed of for over 3 yrs. I eventually opted for surgery, which ended the symptoms for a while and reappeared again. With excruciating pain and intermittent heat waves all over my body that left me disheveled and emotionally troubled beyond description. I went back to the hospital, as the fibroid is now full blown. Another surgery was prescribed; to say I was distraught was the greatest understatement ever." And then a colleague of mine gave a copy of "The Oracle of God devotional." As I browse through the devotional, I came across a testimony of a lady who had similar issue as mine; encouraged by the account, I called the man of God and he prayed for me, placed me on a seven day fast and praying. And he declared I won't need the surgery. And lo and behold, on the sixth day, I noticed a thick discharge coming out of my system. After the fasting period, I went to the hospital for a checkup and there was no a trace of fibroid in me. Glory to God! Sister X. CT.

I may not know what exactly; is the cause of your own weeping, but by the power of the Most High, I destroy that source of pain in your life this day by the reason of the anointing, and it is replaced with joy in Jesus' name. Amen!

Prayer: Every source of sorrow in my life is turned to joy!

April 05th

[ONE YEAR BIBLE PLAN: 1 Samuel 1-3/Luke 8:26-56]

Today's Word: 2 Samuel 5:3-5

I DECREE! I SHALL REIGN IN LIFE!

How old are you? What are your aspirations in life? What is it you desire to accomplish or become in life? Do you desire to make your life count on earth? Or do you just want to live and die unsung?

Saint! What you are today is a product of your desires years ago. What you will become is also a product of your present desires. It is time to begin to take a deeper look at your aspiration. If you are ambitious, then all you now need is boldness. And this day, I release the anointing of boldness upon you in the name of Jesus. Amen!

When the anointing of boldness comes upon you, the intellect, the presence of mind, wisdom and understanding that are requisite for exploit in life rests upon you mightily. David was just a shepherd boy until he was anointed by the Oracle of God, Samuel in [1 Samuel 16]. Afterwards, the capacity to become much more and to do even more, came upon him mightily by the Spirit of God through the anointing. Before long, he became an aide or the Armor bearer to King Saul in [1 Samuel 17]. Then he thereafter, became the King of Judah and then King of the entire nation of Israel. I don't know what your desires are; but this day I release the same anointing that was on David upon you in Jesus' name. Amen!

Prayer: I receive the anointing of boldness to reign in the name of Jesus. Amen!

April 06th

[ONE YEAR BIBLE PLAN: 1 Samuel 4-6/Luke 9:1-17]

Today's Word: Isaiah 43:1-4

THE LORD IS WITH ME IN TIMES OF TROUBLE!

Many times, I have heard Believers profess negative remarks when they face difficulties in life, such as: "God has surely forsaken me"; "I don't think God can solve my problems" etc. This is very unfortunate. If believers would only understand better; the God that we serve, then we'd definitely suffer less.

Saint! You must know that you are precious in the sight of God. [Isaiah 43:4]. Just as you would love to protect something of value, so also God watches over you to protect and preserve you.

Matter of fact, because of His love for you, He is willing to give people' lives in exchange for yours. What a promise! God confirms that as long as you are called by His name, He is duty bound to see you through whatever circumstances you may find yourself. But you must trust Him!

Are you in troubled waters? Are you going through the fire and storm of life? Do you fear that the future is bleak for you and your loved ones? I implore you this day; fear not for the Lord God is with you in the name of Jesus!

God knows every detail of your life. So whatever you are going through now cannot consume you; God will restore you unto glory in Jesus' name. Amen!

Prayer: Father Lord! Equip me to overcome my travails in life in the name of Jesus. Amen!

April 07th

[ONE YEAR BIBLE PLAN: 1 Samuel 7-9/Luke 9:18-36]

Today's Word: 1 Timothy 6:12

I DECREE! I SHALL FIGHT AND WIN THE GOOD FIGHT OF FAITH!

Faith is a fight and the only fight we should fight! And the good news is that you are already declared a winner before the fight start. That is why it is called a good fight. A good fight is one that you win. So, we've been called to fight a good fight where our faith always prevails. Some say the battle is the Lord's and expect God to help them fight their fight of faith. But it is up to you, not God, to fight the fight of faith. It is your fight that will win for you! And you must know that this fight is not with demons. The fight of faith is when you unleash your faith against stubborn situation that contest the integrity of God's Word in your life's circumstances.

You do this by holding on to eternal life; your inheritance in Christ [1 Timothy 6:12]. It didn't say hold on to your Job, to car, or to your house etc. No! It said hold on to eternal life, since you can't see it physically; you do so by a good profession, through faith confessions- by saying the same thing as God about your issues. That is how you fight the good fight of faith. Remember, you can never be disadvantaged or defeated in life because you're more than a conqueror, and the greater One lives in you. Always make this confession daily. I am who God says I am! Glory to God!

Prayer: Lord! Increase me in wisdom and knowledge to fight the good fight of faith in the name of Jesus. Amen!

April 08th

[ONE YEAR BIBLE PLAN: 1 Samuel 10-12/Luke 9:37-62]

Today's Word: Genesis 42:5-10 and Genesis 45:1-9

I DECREE! THE ENEMY WON'T FIND ME WHERE THEY LEFT ME!

They hated Joseph. They could've killed him like Cain did to Abel. But, God did not permit it because He had great plans for him. Then they got rid of him by selling him for twenty pieces of silver. As far as they were concerned, that was the end of him. He had been consigned to a life of obscurity but he became a celebrity; for God was with him. God will be with you through and through in Jesus' name. Amen! Several years afterward, they needed food to survive the biting famine. So they went to Egypt. And there he was! But they could not recognize him. Why? Because he wasn't where they thought he would be. They couldn't have imagined that the boy that they sold into slavery years back had become important; worlds apart from where they left him. He was now governor over the land. Joseph was located by God's Word, and that made the difference between him and his brethren. Today, I send that same Word to you. And I prophesy."The enemy will not find you where they left you!"

They might have put you in the 'pit' of life. They might have ensured that you will never lift up your head. But today, by the anointing of God, I prophesy that the gift that God has bestowed upon you will manifest and cause you to stand before great people like in Joseph. The next time your enemies see you, they will pay you obeisance in Jesus' name!

Prayer:I am coming out of the pit of life in Jesus' name*!*

April 09th

[ONE YEAR BIBLE PLAN: 1 Samuel 13-14/Luke 10:1-24]

WORD SWORD OF THE ORACLE

Today's Word: 2 Chronicles 20:32

*"And he walked in the way of his father Asa, and did not turn aside from it, doing what was **right** in the sight of the Lord."*

RIGHT [HEBREW] 'YASHAR'

The Hebrew word for 'right' is 'Yashar' as used in the verse above and also in [Exodus 15:26; Deuteronomy 12:25; Judges 17:6] Strong's Concordance #3477: This Hebrew word is frequently translated right [as used in the books of Chronicles and Kings to assess the reigns of the kings of Israel and Judah] it is derived from a Hebrew word meaning 'to be level' or 'to be upright.' By extension; it carries the connotations of being just or righteous.

The word is not only used to speak of the perfect righteousness of God [Deuteronomy 32:4; Psalm 111:7-8] but it is also used to speak of the integrity of one's speech [Job 6:25; Ecclesiastes 12:10] or the righteous quality of a person's lifestyle [Proverbs 11:3 and proverbs 11:6].

The word even implies pure and faithful motives as in [Daniel 9:5; 1 Kings 9:5]. As Israel's King David exemplified these qualities in his life [1 Kings 3:6], and became a standard for assessing all the kings that followed him [2 Chronicles 17:3; 2 Chronicles 34:2].

Prayer: Lord! Put a right spirit within me and take not your Holy Spirit from me in Jesus' name. Amen!

Second Sunday of the Month of April

[ONE YEAR BIBLE PLAN: 1 Samuel 15-16/Luke 10:25-42]

CHURCH AND HOME SUNDAY SCHOOL

What is the third baptism that we must experience?

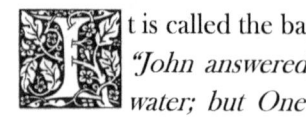t is called the baptism of fire or sanctification. Luke 3:16-17 *"John answered, saying to all, "I indeed baptize you with water; but One mightier than I is coming, whose sandal strap I am not worthy to lose. He will baptize you with the Holy Spirit and fire. His winnowing fan is in His hand, and He will thoroughly clean out His threshing floor, and gather the wheat into His barn; but the chaff He will burn with unquenchable fire."*

WHAT IS THE BAPTISM OF FIRE? It is the process of separation and sanctification employed by God, to bring us into maturity and set us aside for His service. 2 Timothy 2:19-21 *"....the solid foundation of God stands, having this seal: "The Lord knows those who are His," and, "Let everyone who names the name of Christ depart from iniquity." But in a great house there are not only vessels of gold and silver, but also of wood and clay, some for honor and some for dishonor. Therefore if anyone cleanses himself from the latter, he will be a vessel for honor, sanctified and useful for the Master, prepared for every good work."*

<u>Sunday School Question</u>

1) What is the third baptism that we must experience?
2) What is the baptism of fire?

> **Memory Verse:** Luke 3:16 "John answered, saying to all, "I indeed baptize you with water; but One mightier than I is coming, whose sandal strap I am not worthy to lose. He will baptize you with the Holy Spirit and fire."

April 11th

[ONE YEAR BIBLE PLAN: 1 Samuel 17-18/Luke 11:1-28]

Today's Word: Exodus 23:20

"Behold, I send an Angel before you to keep you in the way and to bring you into the place which I have prepared."

GOD WILL LEAD ME TO MY INHERITANCE!

From the beginning of every situation; God knows how it would end. That is why He is Omniscient. He knew the problems the Israelites would face on their way to the Promised Land; so, He sent an angel ahead of them; the angel is mandated to lead and protect them from all the dangers on the journey to the Land of Promise. Eventually, even though it took them forty years, Israel entered into their inheritance as promised by the Lord God!

Saint! The Lord sent me to declare to you that; just like He did for the children of Israel, He has sent an angel to lead you into your inheritance. And favor is the name of your angel, mercy and goodness is the name of your angel. And his duty is to preserve and protect you and your loved ones. He is to lead and direct your steps to your massive breakthrough.

So, henceforth, before you step out, take a few moments to pray this simple prayer: "Angels of the living God go before me and prepare a mighty miracle for me this day in Jesus' name. Amen!"

And I decree! The Lord will lead you to your divine destiny in Jesus' name. Amen!

Prayer: Lord! Lead me to my blessings in Jesus' name. Amen*!*

April 12th

[ONE YEAR BIBLE PLAN: 1 Samuel 19-21/Luke 11:29-54]

Today's Word: Psalm 91:1-5

THE TERROR OF THE NIGHT SHALL NOT HURT ME!

If you are adept at the things of the spirit, or spiritual warfare, you would understand what the scripture refers to as the "terror by night".

It is common knowledge, that night is designed by God for rest. By implication, men should perform their legitimate activities by day and rest at night. But this natural order is not favorable to satanic agents and the kingdom of darkness and wickedness. Due to their clandestine activities, they prefer the cover of night to perpetrate wickedness. It is at night they send evil arrows, projectiles and projections that cause many evil things in the lives of so many people.

Evil projections from the pit of hell manifest in people's life in several ways. For instant, a youth who woke up paralyzed after he was shot in the dream; a lady who woke up with incurable ailment after eating poison in the dream; all these are instances of terror by night.

"While men slept the enemy came to sow tare." At night, all sorts of dark and evil manipulations takes place; but thank God, our protector, will always protect us. Are you of the Lord? If so I decree! By the reason of the anointing the terror of the night will not hurt you and your loved ones in the name of Jesus Christ. Amen!

Prayer: *I* cover my family and myself with the blood of Jesus!

April 13th

[ONE YEAR BIBLE PLAN: 1 Samuel 22-24/Luke 12:1-31]

Today's Word: Amos 9:10-12

I DECREE! THE RAISING UP OF ALL MY RUINS!

Saint! You may be experiencing one difficulty or the other right now resulting, from past errors in decisions making, actions or inactions. Your life may be a stale tale of upheavals and disasters right now. You may be at the lowest level of life today; but change is coming your way for good this time in Jesus' name. Amen! I come to declare God's counsel to you this day; fear not and be not dismay for the Lord will raise you up, higher than your wildest dream or expectation in Jesus' name. Amen!

Failures are never finals. The determinant of the outcome of failure in anyone's life is the mindset and reaction of the person to his or her situation. If you have a 'never say die' attitude, you will always emerge from that dungeon of failure to enormous success.

When David lost everything at Ziklag in [1 Samuel 30], it seem as though his end has come. But his mindset, his champion spirit, and attitude took absolute control of him. So, he encouraged himself in the Lord and took a step of faith that resulted in him recovery more that all he had lost. I prophesy, the Lord will grant you the courage to discover yourself so that you can recover all you've lost in Jesus' name. Amen! Like David you will recover all in Jesus' name. Amen!

Prayer: O God of David, rebuild every broken and fallen aspect of life, make me whole again in Jesus' name. Amen!

April 14th

[ONE YEAR BIBLE PLAN: 1 Samuel 25-26/Luke 12:32-59]

Today's Word: Matthew 21:18-22

I DECREE! EVERY SEED OF UNFRUITFULNESS IN MY LIFE IS WITHERED!

Most times, in the bible, trees are metaphors for men. So, Jesus' encounter with the fig tree in our text-passage above; is an indirect lesson to man. Just like He did for the fig tree, God expects us to be fruitful.

So, whenever and wherever our life does not bear fruit, it is in negation to God's desire for us. That is why Jesus cursed that fig tree in anger. Is there a fruitless tree in your life?

Saint! You can change that situation with the words of your mouth. If you are distraught with your situation, you can decree an end to it just like Jesus did. Just rise up now and begin to command every unfruitful situation in your life to wither now in the name of Jesus Christ. Amen!

God created us in His own image and charged us to be fruitful and multiply [Genesis 1:28]. Is there any part of your life that is not fruitful? Have you come short of your expectations in life? If so, I like you to know that it is a demonic manifestation. As the Oracle of God, I decree! Every fruitless tree in your life is withered now in the mighty name of Jesus. Amen!

Prayer: Lord Jesus! Every unfruitful tree in my life I command them now to wither now in the name of Jesus Christ. Amen!

April 15th

[ONE YEAR BIBLE PLAN: 1 Samuel 27-29 /Luke 13:1-22]

Today's Word: Matthew 14:15-21

"....He took the five loaves and the two fish, and looking up to heaven, He blessed and broke and gave the loaves to the disciples; and the disciples gave to the multitudes. So they all ate and were filled, and they took up twelve baskets full of the fragments..."

I DECREE! I SHALL HAVE SURPLUS SUPPLY!

In the text-passage above, Jesus used the miracle of feeding more than five thousand people to teach us; two of the most potent keys of supernatural increase, and for us to recognize God as the source of all things. They were at the middle of the desert with only five loaves of bread and two fishes and more than five thousand mouths to be fed. Humanly speaking that was an impossibility; that is why Jesus' disciples suggested that the crowd be dispersed. But Lo and Behold! As Jesus looked up and gave thanks to God, the food became more than sufficient. Glory to God!

You can use this same principle to change your adverse situation. Instead of fretting over problems, instead of seeing all the reason why everything in your life is not working out well for you. Instead of blaming the world for your situation, just begin to acknowledge and appreciate God as your source of supply. You can make it more practical by blessing whatever little substance you have and as you do so, the Lord God of Israel will multiply what you have now which is barely enough to become more than enough in Jesus' name!

Prayer: Lord Jesus! I look up to you in acknowledgment and appreciation of all You have provided! Thank You Lord*!*

April 16th

[ONE YEAR BIBLE PLAN: 1 Samuel 30-31/Luke 13:23-35]

WORD SWORD OF THE ORACLE

Today's Word: 2 Chronicles 29:16

---

*"Then the priests went into the inner part of the house of the Lord to **cleanse** it, and brought out all the debris that they found in the temple of the Lord to the court of the house of the Lord. And the Levites took it out and carried it to the Brook Kidron."*

CLEANSE [HEBREW] 'TAHER'

'Taher' is the Hebrew word for 'cleanse' as used in the above text and in [Lev. 14:48, Ps. 51:2, Ps. 51:7, Is. 66:17]. This term means 'to make free from blemish,' almost always in a ritual or spiritual sense; although for once; the word is used for the wind's clearing away of clouds and once also for refiner's purifying of silver, [Job 37:21, Mal. 3:3]. Almost half the occurrences of this word are in Leviticus, where ritual cleansing is related to sanctification and is opposed to moral filthiness of the Israelites [Lev. 16:19]. Objects and people involved in the worship of God: such as temple, furniture in the temple, and the Levites- needed cleansing because God is Holy [Num. 8:5-22, 1 Chr. 23:28]. The ritual external cleansing of people was a symbol of internal purity [Gen. 35:2, Zech. 3:3-5].

Jeremiah and Ezekiel prophesied of the future cleansing of God's people, both outside and inside [Jer. 33:8, Ezek. 36:25, Ezek. 36:33, Ezek. 37:23]. This idea carries through into the N.T. The Book of Revelation pictures the Lamb's bride; the Church; in clean linen which symbolizes our righteous acts [2 Cor. 7:1, Eph. 5:26, 1 John 1:9 and Rev. 19:8].

Third Sunday of the Month of April

[ONE YEAR BIBLE PLAN: 2 Samuel 1-2/ Luke 14:1-24]

CHURCH AND HOME SUNDAY SCHOOL

Why is it called "the baptism of fire"?

It is called Baptism of fire because through it the flame of God's love is fanned within us. Luke 3:17 *"His winnowing fan is in His hand, and He will thoroughly clean out His threshing floor, and gather the wheat into His barn; but the chaff He will burn with unquenchable fire."*

2 Timothy 2:19-20 *"Nevertheless the solid foundation of God stands, having this seal: "The Lord knows those who are His," and, "Let everyone who names the name of Christ depart from iniquity." But in a great house there are not only vessels of gold and silver, but also of wood and clay, some for honor and some for dishonor."*

HOW CAN WE LEARN MORE ABOUT THE "BAPTISM OF FIRE"?

We can learn more about the Baptism of fire as we get to studying Sanctification in subsequent studies. 2 Timothy 2:21

<u>Sunday School Question</u>

1) Why is it called "the baptism of fire"?
2) How can we learn more about the "baptism of fire"?

> Memorize: 2 Timothy 2:21 "Therefore if anyone cleanses himself from the latter, he will be a vessel for honor, sanctified and useful for the Master, prepared for every good work."

April 18th

[ONE YEAR BIBLE PLAN: 2 Samuel 3-5/ Luke 14:25-35]

Today's Word: Mark 11:1-2

I WILL BE DIVINELY LOCATED FOR FAVOR!

I am sure there was more than one colt that was tied in the village court referred to in the above scripture. But, Jesus sent the disciples to release the colt in our text-passage. Such is the workings of divine location. Divine location is the act of picking someone/something out from the crowd for exaltation or blessings by God or His representative. It is not subject to merit; it is but a product of divine providence. When a person is divinely located, he/she moves from a position of obscurity and inconsequence to stardom and prominence. That is exactly what happened to the colt in the text-passage above.

As soon as Jesus Christ sent His disciples to lose it from bondage, it became a celebrity; which had to walk on precious garments as it carried the King of Kings, the Lord of lords and the King of glory [Mark 11:5-8]. Whatever it is you're going through right now? I want you to know that Jesus is very much aware of it. You may think that you are lowly, lonely and unimportant, but the truth is that you are very important in God's plan. So, He has decided to lift you up this day. In order to do this, He asked me to declare His Word over your life. Therefore, on the authority of that command, I prophesy that this is your season of divine location. Jesus will locate you for a breakthrough miracle this time in Jesus' gracious name. Amen!

Prayer: O God! Single me out for a breakthrough miracle this day in the name of Jesus. Amen!!

April 19th

[ONE YEAR BIBLE PLAN: 2 Samuel 6-8/ Luke 15:1-10]

Today's Word: Matthew 23:11 and Matthew 20:20-28

I DECREE! I SHALL BE TRULY GREAT!

Our sense, no matter how objective, will still remain inadequate because we're limited in knowledge, understanding and ability to know the future. Many rich people have no future. Most will become so impoverished that you will wonder if they were ever rich. God is the greatest; so He only can call you into true greatness. He called us to become great, as He promised Abraham in [Genesis 12:1-3]. Becoming great, God's ways differs from, and are sometimes even at variance with ours. For instance, those we assume will make it in life are the most brilliant, most talented, most educated; people born with golden spoons in their mouths. Yet God sees a man who does not have any of these qualities and says, 'You will be great' and it is so! Saint! You must seek greatness God's way. Any position you fight for and succeed in obtaining by your strength without God; will cause you aches and pains! But when you seek promotion from God and get it, He sustains it. For God to be involved in your elevation, you must serve others as you serve. And that will get you to a higher position in God's Kingdom. Invest your time, resources and intellect in His Kingdom. Spend and be spent for Jesus. God is not unrighteous to forget your labor of love.

What do you do when you aspire to get a position at your job, at school or even in church? Do you blackmail others to replace them? These are carnal steps to greatness. Separate from such sin and as you do I prophesy the Lord God will bring you to greatness in Jesus' name. Amen!

April 20th

[ONE YEAR BIBLE PLAN: 2 Samuel 9-11/ Luke 15:11-32]

Today's Word: 2 Corinthians 4:13

MY FAITH ATTITUDE SHALL BRING ME VICTORY!

As a believer, you must have a different attitude than others in the world. It is the attitude of faith that will bring you victory. That is what Paul connotes as the spirit of faith. You must have the same spirit as the apostles and those in the hall of faith in Book of [Hebrews 11]. It is by this spirit of faith that you know you can't be defeated; you can't be broken, you can't remain sick and poor in life. Come what may; by this spirit you always out-shine darkness and walk in victory.

You must develop this mindset and make it a habit of declaring faith-filled Words about your life's situation. Speak God's Word over your circumstances and see them change for good. Speak prosperity into everything you do in life and prosper thereby. This is the principle; God used in creation; He spoke forth what He believed. He said "Let there be light" and light came into being. He spoke to chaos to bring order! He released Word of faith for creation. Always speak in line with God's Word. Never talk yourself down! Never speak failure, defeat or lack! Never ever talk sickness but talk health and wealth always. Amen! You have God's life in you that should destroy infirmity and afflictions. So, it does not matter how you feel or what you feel now because God is real in you more than what your feel. Maintain this attitude and you will reap the victory of the faith attitude in all your endeavors!

Prayer: Lord! Grant me the grace to maintain the faith attitude in Jesus' name. Amen!

April 21st

[ONE YEAR BIBLE PLAN: 2 Samuel 12-13/ Luke 16]

Today's Word: Psalm 126:1-end

I DECREE! I SHALL LAUGH LAST!

Psalm 126 says *"When the Lord turned again the captivity of Zion; we were like them that dream..."* There are miracles that when you have them you will think you are dreaming. And you're going to get plenty of such miracles this season in Jesus' name. *"...Then was our mouth filled with laughter."* God will fill your mouth with laughter! *"....and our tongue with singing"!* This season you are going to praises God. *"...then, said they among the heathen, the Lord hath done great things for them.* Unbelievers will testify that God has been good to you in Jesus' name. *"...The Lord hath done great things for us; whereof we are glad. Turn again our captivity, O Lord, as the streams in the south. They that sow in tears shall reap in joy. He that goeth forth and weeping, bearing precious seed shall doubtless come again with rejoicing, bringing his sheaves with him."* I want you to declare thus: "I SHALL LAUGH LAST IN JESUS' NAME".

When we talk about laughter; laughter can be in several forms and categories; there is the laughter of mockery, there is the laughter of joy, there is the laughter of the enemy, there is the laughter of a friend who is rejoicing with you, but probably the best laughter of all is the 'last laugh'. It doesn't matter how long the enemies have been laughing at you, you will laugh last in the name of Jesus. Alleluia! Glory to God!

Prayer: Lord! Make me laugh last in the name of Jesus!

April 22nd

[ONE YEAR BIBLE PLAN: 2 Samuel 14-15/ Luke 17:1-20]

Today's Word: Deuteronomy 8:18

I RECEIVE THE POWER TO MAKE WEALTH!

When God gives a charge; He usually backs it up with confirmation. Early this year, the Lord gave me a mandate to raise millionaires for Him; who would lift up and spread the gospel. As the Oracle of God, the Lord has endued me with the power to make you wealthy. 2 Chronicles 20:20 says *"....Believe in the Lord your God, and you shall be established; believe His prophets, and you shall prosper".* By divine principle, I can only release this power on you through prophetic declarations. After which, it is left for you to believe, receive and achieve it, as God confirms it. So, I decree unto your life now; the power to make wealth is hereby released upon you in the name of Jesus. Amen!

As a matter of obligation, I have declared God's mind, concerning you to you. Now accept it, by believing it and cooperate with it; you will receive and achieve it in Jesus' name. Amen! Know that God cannot lie! And He is a God of purpose and He is committed to His purpose. Once He says a thing, He works assiduously to see that it is done. You are one of the millionaires to be raised this year in Jesus' name. Amen! I am confident because, the God that sent me to prophesy unto you is the One that gives power to be wealthy. So, I admonish you; receive the power to make wealth now in Jesus' name. Amen!

Prayer: Lord! Give me the grace to receive the power to make wealth in the name of Jesus. Amen!

April 23rd

[ONE YEAR BIBLE PLAN: 2 Samuel 16-18/ Luke 17:20-37]

WORD SWORD OF THE ORACLE

Today's Word: 2 Chronicles 31:5

---

*"As soon as the commandment was circulated, the children of Israel brought in abundance the first-fruits of grain and wine, oil and honey, and of all the produce of the field; and they brought in abundantly the **tithe** of everything."*

TITHE [HEBREW] 'MA'ASER'

'Ma'aser' is the Hebrew word for 'tithe' as used in our text-verse above and also in [2 Chronicles 31:12, Genesis 14:20, Malachi 3:10.] Strong's Concordance #4643:

The Hebrew word translated tithe is derived from the word 'eser; the Hebrew word for number ten.

In [Genesis 14:20], Abraham gave Priest Melchizedek a tenth of all his wealth. This set the precedent throughout the Old Testament for what was considered appropriate portion of one's wealth to give to God. According to law, Israelites were to set aside a tenth of their annual produce for God [Deuteronomy 14:22-28].

Whatever was given to God was considered holy; [Leviticus 27:30-33] and was to be used to support the ministry of the Priests and Levites [Numbers 18:21]. Prophet Malachi proclaimed that the failure to bring the entire tithe to God was the equivalent of robbing Him. [Malachi 3:8-10].

Prayer: O Lord My Father! Grant me the grace to tithe in the name of Jesus. Amen!

Fourth Sunday of the Month of April

[ONE YEAR BIBLE PLAN: 2 Samuel 19-20/ Luke 18:1-23]

CHURCH AND HOME SUNDAY SCHOOL

What is the doctrine of laying-on of hands?

It is the belief that divine power or qualities can be transferred from one believer to another by laying hands upon the head of an individual by a more anointed individual. Acts 8:17 *"Then they laid hands on them, and they received the Holy Spirit."* See also [Acts 5:12; Hebrews 7:7]

WHY DO WE STUDY THE MINISTRY OR DOCTRINE OF THE LAYING-ON OF HANDS?

The laying on of hands is presented in the Bible as one of the principle of the Doctrine of Christ. Hebrews 6:1-2 *"Therefore, leaving the discussion of the elementary principles of Christ, let us go on to perfection, not laying again the foundation of repentance from dead works and of faith toward God, of the doctrine of baptisms, of laying on of hands, of resurrection of the dead, and of eternal judgment."*

<u>Sunday School Question</u>

1) What is the doctrine of laying-on of hands?
2) Why do we study the ministry or doctrine of the laying on of hands?

> **Memory Verse:** Mark 16:17-18 "... these signs will follow ...: In My name ...; they will speak with new tongues; ...and if they drink anything deadly, it will by no means hurt them; they will lay hands on the sick, and they will recover."

April 25th

[ONE YEAR BIBLE PLAN: 2 Samuel 21-22/ Luke 18:24-43]

Today's Word: Hebrews 4:14-16

I SHALL OBTAIN GOD'S GRACE AND MERCY!

This following testimony will edify you please read on:

"*Last January I was diagnosed with fibroid, and was really troubled. My concern was heightened when I was scheduled for surgery. I had no money, and no medical insurance, no Medicare, Medicaid or Obamacare; none whatsoever! However, fully aware of the full implication of the death of Jesus Christ on the cross of Calvary, I decided not go for the surgery. Instead, my husband and I beseeched God in prayer and fasting; we prayer for God's mercy and grace upon me on the prayer conference of the Oracle of God. A few weeks afterwards, the symptoms ceased; so I went to the surgeon for check up. Lo and Behold the fibroid was gone to the amazement of the medical staff. I thank God for His mighty deliverance upon my life."* Sister Anita Cole. NY, NY.

Saint! What is the sickness that the enemy has planted in you? What is the devourer in your family that is the cause for financial concern in your life? I like you to know now that Jesus Christ is a compassionate high priest who is touched by your affliction. And He is willing and able to heal and deliver you as He did for the sister in the above praise report. He said call upon me and I will answer you. Do you have issues in your life? Call on Jesus Christ in faith, in fasting and in prayer. As you do, I decree you shall obtain God's mercy!

Prayer: O God of mercy deliver me from all my afflictions!

April 26th

[ONE YEAR BIBLE PLAN: 2 Sam. 2:23-24/ Luke 19:1-27]

Today's Word: 2 Kings 6:1-2

GOD WILL DIVINELY INSPIRE ME FOR SUCCESS!

More often than not, achievers are self-inspired individuals. If you don't have this quality, you will be at best an average individual. When you are self-inspired, you don't rest on the oars of one level; but you move from one achievement to the other in great successions without prompting; in leaps and bounds. If the sons of the prophet in the above text were not inspired to seek a better dwelling place, they would have continued in that strait condition all their lives; managing their place of abode. But as they were inspired; they went beyond their present level.

Many do not get greater results in life due to their inability to inspire themselves; they are content with their situations. As soon as they are able to make ends meet, able to feed themselves and their families, they stop aspiring higher. This is a major issue that has left many in poverty. I admonish you this day to evaluate your achievement quotient right now.

Are you content with just getting along? If you are, I implore you to change your thinking and your life will change accordingly. '....For as a man thinketh in his heart so he is'. The bible says. Know this day that God created you to be outstanding and to manifest His glory; you must be self-inspired attain this. So, I decree divine inspiration and insight upon you now in Jesus' name. Amen!

Prayer: Lord! Let me be inspired to achieve greater success!

April 27th

[ONE YEAR BIBLE PLAN: 1 Kings 1-2/ Luke 19:28-48]

Today's Word: Luke 4:1-15

I SHALL OVERCOME THE TRIALS OF LIFE!

Many at times, when faced with challenges of life, many tend to ask in frustration: why me? Why now? Am I the only one? Etc. If you're one of such people, listen to the words of Robert Browning; he said *"'WHY' comes from temptations, but for man to meet, master and make crouch beneath his foot, and so be pedestaled in triumph."* In other words, he is saying temptations are like test or exams that precede promotions. So, when next you face a challenge; instead of crying and complaining, see it as an opportunity to move to the next higher level in life. Constant challenges are opportunities for advancement and those who are afraid of them never make considerable progress in life. If Jesus, the Son of God faced challenges; there is no reason why man should not or would not. Test leads to testimony; no test no money! No trial, no triumph, no obstacles no miracles! Christ countenance and reaction throughout His temptation proved that Jesus knew that temptation was a precondition for the establishment of His ministry on earth. That position was justified by the instant lifting that followed His victory over Satan. [Luke 14:15]. Have you been overwhelmed by the challenges in your life? Saint! Just trust in the Lord and He will see you through. You will overcome the trials of life in Jesus' name. As you overcome one challenge after the other, you will greatly advance in Jesus' name. Amen!

Prayer: Lord! Give me the grace to overcome trials!

April 28th

[ONE YEAR BIBLE PLAN: 1 Kings 3-5/ Luke 20:1-26]

Today's Word: Esther 6:4-10

I SHALL BE EXALTED IN THE PRESENCE OF MY ENEMIES!

When the Psalmist in [Psalm 23:5], observed that God prepares a table for His beloved in the presence of their enemies he sure knew what he was talking about. Indeed, God has a great sense of humor.

Or else, how can the above scenario in our text passage above be imagined; that mighty Haman, the King's Chief Chamberlain was made to chaperon Mordecai, a lowly gatekeeper whom he desired more than anything else to hang on the gallows.

Saint! Who is it that has become a thorn in your flesh? Is it an envious colleague, supervisor, manager "a damager"? Is it your boss? Who are those that have decree that you will only prosper over their dead bodies? Is household wickedness or in-laws and "out-laws" working relentlessly against your progress? I prophesy you shall be exalted above all the Hamans in your life in the name of Jesus!

As you receive this prophecy now, something is already happening in the realm of the spirit; causing a shift in your favor in the mighty name of Jesus. Amen! You shall be lifted on the shoulders of your enemies in Jesus' name. Amen!

Prayer: O God of Mordecai! I call upon you now; prepare a table for me in the presence of my enemies in Jesus' mighty name. Amen!

April 29th

[ONE YEAR BIBLE PLAN: 1 Kings 6-7/ Luke 20:27-47]

Today's Word: Ezekiel 18:1-20

I SHALL NO LONGER SUFFER FOR THE SINS OF MY FATHERS!

In Exodus 20:5, God established a statue with Israel. As time pass, this Covenant became a societal norm in the land. It was under the reign of the law that God passed judgments of death and destruction on the children of David in [2 Samuel 12]. And on Ahab in [1 Kings 21] etc; their children suffered for their father's sins. And the proverb ensued *"the fathers have eaten grapes and the children's teeth are on edge."* However, as the dispensation of grace set in, God removed the pain of the Law.

In [Jeremiah 31:28-30 and Ezekiel 18], God revealed to His prophets that when grace is poured out, every man will be judged according to their own conduct. The death of Jesus finally established that New Covenant.

But 2000 years after, the devil still held men bound under his throes with the statues of the law. This is only possible because of ignorance. Have you accepted the problems of your life as consequence of the sins and deeds of your fathers?

Saint! The only condition that your father's sin will affect you is that you are actively committing sin. As long as you give your life to Jesus Christ, you have the right of the New Covenant. Are you sure you are born again? Then pray thus:

Prayer: Lord! I rededicate my life to you this day; Holy Spirit give me the grace to continue in you in Jesus' name. Amen!

April 30th

[ONE YEAR BIBLE PLAN: 1 Kings 8-8/ Luke 21:1-19]]

WORD SWORD OF THE ORACLE

Today's Word: 2 Chronicles 30:1

*"And Hezekiah sent to all Israel and Judah, and also wrote letters to Ephraim and Manasseh, that they should come to the house of the Lord at Jerusalem, to keep the **Passover** to the Lord God of Israel."*

PASSOVER [HEBREW] 'PESACH'

The Hebrew word for 'Passover' is 'Pesach' as used above and in [Exodus 12:11, Exodus 12:43, Ezekiel 45:21]. Strong's #6453: Passover is derived from the Hebrew word meaning "to pass" or "to leap over." The festival was named thus; because it commemorated the time when God spared the first born of the Israelites, who sprinkled the blood from the Passover lamb on their doorpost. God "passed over" the families so designated, not visiting their households with death [Exodus 12]. So that the Israelites would not forget God's mercy on them; the Law of Moses prescribed in detail the ritual for commemorating the Passover [Leviticus 23:5-8, Numbers 28:16-25, Deuteronomy 16:1-8]. King Hezekiah's great Passover signaled spiritual renewal in Judah, including the removal of sin and impurity [2 Chronicles 30:14], joyful praise for God's pardon [2 Chronicles 30:21-22], and a prolonged celebration of God's blessings [2 Chronicles 30:23-26].

Later Jesus celebrated this feast with His disciples [Matthew 26:2, Matthew 26:18], and in His death and resurrection; He became its fulfillment, the ultimate Passover Lamb for our sins [John 1:29, 1 Corinthians 5:7, 1 Peter 1:19].

First Sunday of the Month of May

[ONE YEAR BIBLE PLAN: 1 Kings 10-11/ Luke 21:20-38]

CHURCH AND HOME SUNDAY SCHOOL

Was the laying-on of hands practiced in the Old Testament?

es! This doctrine was practiced for various reasons and occasions:1. The priest laid their hands on the scapegoat to transfer to it the sins of the people.

Leviticus 16:21-22 *"Aaron shall lay both his hands on the head of the live goat, confess over it all the iniquities of the children of Israel, and all their transgressions, concerning all their sins, putting them on the head of the goat, and shall send it away into the wilderness by the hand of a suitable man."*

2. Jacob placed his hands upon Joseph's children to convey his blessings on them.

Genesis 48:14 *"Then Israel stretched out his right hand and laid it on Ephraim's head, who was the younger, and his left hand on Manasseh's head, guiding his hands knowingly, for Manasseh was the firstborn."*

3. Moses conferred a portion of his wisdom and spirit upon the elders. Numbers 27:18-23

Sunday School Question

1) Was laying-on of hand practiced in the Old Testament?

Memory Verse: Hebrews 7:7 "Now beyond all contradiction the lesser is blessed by the better."

May 02nd

[ONE YEAR BIBLE PLAN: 1 Kings 12-13/ Luke 22:1-30]

Today's Word: Jeremiah 33:11

THE GRACE TO PRAISE GOD IS UPON ME!

Praise is an expression of your faith in God, a declaration of victory in Christ Jesus! When you praise God, you are indeed declaring your believe and total trust in God. I prophesy as you praise and worship the Lord today, He will cause you to return from bondage in Jesus' name. Amen!

PRAISE GOD NOW!

You are the Lord of Hosts! The I AM THAT I AM! The Rock of Ages! The Unchangeable Lord! The Ancient of Days! I Magnify Your Holy Name! Your Name is wonderful, Counselor! Mighty God! The Everlasting Father! The Prince of Peace! I Praise and Worship You O Lord! You are the Lion of the Tribe of Judah! The Rose of Sharon! The Lily of the Valley! You are worthy to be praised and worshiped so I worship you in Jesus' name. Amen!

MAY BIRTHDAY AND WEDDING ANNIVERSARY PRAYERS!

Father, thank You for all Your children born in the month of May and those celebrating any anniversary this month. May is the fifth month of the year and number five is the number of grace: Father God deal graciously with them. As they start a new year, grant them new joy, new blessings, and new successes. Lord, they will not be deprived of marital bliss and blessings. In every area of their lives, Lord be gracious unto them in Jesus' mighty Name. Amen!

May 03rd

[ONE YEAR BIBLE PLAN: 1 Kings 14-15/ Luke 22:31-46]

Today's Word: 2 Kings 6:13-23

GOD WILL FRUSTRATE ALL THAT SEEK MY HURT!

It is a dangerous thing to be against the anointed of God. King Saul; Saul who became Apostle Paul and many more in Scripture and in this time and age; learnt their lesson the hard way. Had the King of Syria and his men knew better; they would not have attempted to go against the anointing: but they did and suffered?

Saint, know this day that you are a child of God and as such you are His anointed. And no power can prevail over you! Our God neither sleeps nor slumber, He is watching over you to protect and preserve you. And He also wants to show Himself mighty on your behalf, so for this same reason he had to fulfill the counsel of Prophet Elisha, and made the captor become the captive by making the adversary blind at the word of Elisha. Consequently, Elisha who should be begging for mercy was now positioned to show mercy to the enemy.

I don't know who the foe and adversary in your life is right now; but I do know that the good Lord is working behind the scene to turn the situation around in your favor in Jesus' mighty name. Amen! Your enemies will be forced to swallow their pride this time; they will alight from their high horse and be at your mercy in Jesus' name. Amen! If you believe and agree with me then pray this prayer all day today.

Prayer: O Lord! Make me prevail over my foes and adversaries in Jesus' name. Amen!

May 04th

[ONE YEAR BIBLE PLAN: 1 Kings 16-18/ Luke 22:47-71]

Today's Word: James 2:19-21

I AM MOVING FROM JUST BELIEVING TO FAITH!

Believing is not faith and Faith does not just believe; faith believes with added action. Faith is not passive, faith is active. When you receive the Word of God into your heart and believe what it says, that is just the first step in the equation; there must be corresponding action to whatever you believed. For instant, Romans 10:10 says *"For with the heart one believes unto righteousness, and with the mouth confession is made unto salvation."* So, when you heard the gospel and you were convicted in your heart to believe Jesus died for you, you were made right with God. But that wouldn't have gotten you born again: there had to be a corresponding action of confession that catapults you unto salvation. No matter how much you may have cried, prayed and thank God for sending His Son to die for you, if you hadn't taken the step to declare it, you would not have experience salvation. The principle is the same for every other aspect of your Christian life. You must not stop at merely accepting what the Word says; you must take a step further by making confession or taking further action. Faith is a leap on the Word of God. It is believing what God's Word says concerning anything, and acting that way. For the one who was sick, faith will cause him/her to declare that he/she was healed by the stripe of Jesus and then begin to move himself/herself, even if slowly at first. For faith to be faith, and not just believing; it's got to have some action. I prophesy you are moving from just believing to faith in Jesus' name. Amen!

May 05th

[ONE YEAR BIBLE PLAN: 1 Kings 19-20/ Luke 23:1-25]

Today's Word: Exodus 23:27

I DECREE! THIS DAY MY ENEMIES SHALL TURN BACK AND FLEE!

If there is one testimony you should claim, it is that your enemy should turn and flee from you! Do you understand the implication of the decree above? Then, you must say a resounding Amen to it! This is because there is more to this prophecy than meets the eyes. Come to think of it; what do you think it means for your enemies to turn their backs to you? For a clear understanding, imagine that life is a battlefield. And imagine that during the course of a battle, your opponents suddenly turned their backs at you and flee. What does this mean? It means your enemy is defeat! It means victory for you! It means that the enemy could no longer continue with the fight so they fled for their lives. By implication, they are acknowledging that they've lost the battle. I pray that is the portion of your enemy this day in the name of Jesus!

I decree! Your enemies shall turn and flee from you in the name of Jesus. As the Lord God liveth, situations, occasions, instance that appear challenging; confronting you this year; as you stand your ground and declare the Word of God to them, they shall disperse and scatter, they shall give up and flee from you in Jesus' name. Amen!

Prayer: I decree I shall see the back of my enemies as they flee from me in Jesus' name. Amen!

May 06th

[ONE YEAR BIBLE PLAN: 1 Kings 21-22/ Luke 23:26-56]

Today's Word: John 15:1-6

I SHALL NOT BE CAST OUT FROM GOD'S PRESENCE!

The worst thing that can happen to you is to be cast out of God's presence. In our text-passage above, Jesus used the relationship between a tree trunk and its branch to illustrate His relationship with man. According Him, just like a branch that is cut away from the trunk withers with time, a man that is separated from God is gradually destroyed. Such was the case of King Saul.

As soon as God abandoned him, he lost peace, direction and boldness [1 Samuel 15]. Consequently, the same Saul anointed king by God, who banished witchcraft practices in the Land of Israel began to consult witches for direction. Judas was another man who was cast out from God's presence. His case was even more pitiable.

For over three years, he followed Jesus Christ. He saw the miracles the Master did, he wined and dined with Him, he even performed miracles himself when Jesus sent them out. Yet, because of greed, he lost his place in eternity. I don't know who you are or what you do, but I stand in the gap for you, and decree that you will not be cast out of God's presence in Jesus' name. Amen! Whatever you do and in whatever situation you find yourself, endeavor to remain connected with God. You can do this by first giving your life to Jesus that is; if you have not yet done so, and then maintain fellowship and obey Him. Remain Blessed!

May 07th

[ONE YEAR BIBLE PLAN: 2 Kings 1-3/ Luke24:1-35]

WORD SWORD OF THE ORACLE

Today's Word: Ezra 5:1

---

*"Then the prophet Haggai and Zechariah the son of Iddo, prophets, prophesied to the **Jews** who were in Judah and Jerusalem, in the name of the God of Israel, who was over them."*

JEW [HEBREW] 'YEHUDI'

'Yehudi' is the Hebrew word for 'Jew' as used in the above text-verse and also in [Ezra 6:7 and Daniel 3:8] Strong's Concordance #3062:

The name 'Jew' is popularly associated with the verb 'Yadah' which means 'to praise' or 'to give thanks' on the basis of Jacob's blessing upon his son Judah in [Genesis 49:8] on his deathbed. He said "Judah you are he whom your brothers shall praise." Thus a 'Jew' may be a person from the tribe of Judah [Numbers 10:14].

Later the name Jew was applied directly to those Israelites living in the geographical region known as Judah See [Jeremiah 7:30].

The name 'Jew' for the Israelites as a people became prominent during the postexilic period. This use is found in the New Testament as well: Jesus is called "the King of the Jews" [Matthew 27:29].

In his letter to the Romans, Paul the Apostle, states that the true 'Jew' is a person mark by "circumcision of the heart" [Romans 2:28-29]. Praise God!

Second Sunday of the Month of May

[ONE YEAR BIBLE PLAN: 2 Kings 4-6/ Luke 24:36-53]

CHURCH AND HOME SUNDAY SCHOOL

WAS THE LAYING ON OF HANDS PRACTICED IN THE NEW TESTAMENT?

Yes! The laying on of hands was practiced by Jesus Christ and His followers.

1. Jesus laid hands upon the sick to heal them. [Luke 4:40]

2. The Apostles laid hands on the sick and they were healed. Acts 28:8 *"And it happened that the father of Publius lay sick of a fever and dysentery. Paul went in to him and prayed, and he laid his hands on him and healed him."*

3. True believers in Jesus Christ have authority to lay hands on the sick for healing. Mark 16:17-18 *"And these signs will follow those who believe: In My name they will cast out demons; they will speak with new tongues; 18 they[a] will take up serpents; and if they drink anything deadly, it will by no means hurt them; they will lay hands on the sick, and they will recover."*

4. Jesus laid His hands upon the children to bless them. Mark 10:16 *"And He took them up in His arms, laid His hands on them, and blessed them."*

<u>Sunday school question</u>

1) Was the laying on of hands in the n. t.?

Memory Verse: Mark 16:18 "They will take up serpents; and if theydrink anything deadly, it will by no means hurt them; they will lay hands on the sick, and they will recover."

May 09th

[ONE YEAR BIBLE PLAN: 2 Kings 7-9/ John 1:1-28]

Today's Word: Psalm 34:1-6

GOD SHALL DELIVER ME FROM ALL MY TROUBLES!

"*Couple of months ago, my marriage began to experience upheavals. I discerned that something wasn't just right. As my husband had begun to keep late nights and tell lies. I just knew that all was not well. And the more I confront him, the more difficult the situation became. So, I called Pastor Stevie Okauru, who confirmed my fears and concern. He said there was a strange woman in the picture. With his counsel, fasting and praying; to the glory of God in seven day as declare by the Oracle of God! Without any prompting whatsoever, my husband confessed his involvement in an affair with another woman. He asked for my forgiveness and promised not to ever misbehave again. He has since changed and peace is been restore to my family. I thank the Lord for delivering my family!* Sister Irena Baltimore MD.

Are you in a similar situation? Has the appearance of a strange woman or man diverted the attention of your spouse away from you? Has lack brought strain upon your relationship? Are you experiencing any kind of problem in your home, your job place or business? Saint! There is solution only in Jesus Christ! All you need to do is to present the case to Him with a heart of faith. True to His reputation, He will take care of that adverse situation speedily. Pray thus:

Prayer: By the reason of the anointing I see all my adversities crumble in the name of Jesus. Amen!

May 10th

[ONE YEAR BIBLE PLAN: 2 Kings 10-12/ John 1:29-51]

Today's Word: Mark 7:31-35

I DECREE! THIS IS MY SEASON OF OPEN DOORS!

Is there any closed door in your life? Is there any area of your life that you remember with a tinge of anxiety? Is it your marriage? Is it in the area of finance? Or your education, career, health etc., whatever it is; I admonish you to perform the following spiritual exercise by faith right now: look up to heaven and decree thus: "Every closed door in my life, I speak to you now, Ephphatha! Be opened in the name of Jesus. Amen! If you have done so, then receive it now in the name of Jesus! I decree! This is your season of open doors!

Saint! Whenever and wherever Jesus desired to do a great miracle, He looked up to heaven and gave thanks. That was what happened with the raising of Lazarus from the dead in [John 11], also in the case of feeding more than five thousand people in [Matthew 14]. By so doing, Jesus simply showed that heaven is the original source of all good things; every other source is just a resource. What was obtainable then is still obtainable now. I've looked up to heaven on your behalf and have secured a release of blessing upon you this day. So, as God's Oracle, I decree this is your season of open doors in the name of Jesus. Amen! In your career, your marriage, your business, education, finance, health, etc., receive now divinely opened doors in Jesus' name. Amen!

Prayer: Lord I look up to You! Open all my closed doors in the name of Jesus. Amen!

May 11th

[ONE YEAR BIBLE PLAN: 2 Kings 13-14/ John 2]

Today's Word: 2 Chronicles 33:1-13

GOD SHALL HEAR MY SUPPLICATIONS THIS TIME!

We all have the propensity to live our lives against the dictates of God. But when we notice that we have erred and return to Him; God is forever willing to forgive and cleanse us from all unrighteousness. For God does not despise a broken and contrite heart. Manasseh was a radical deviation from his father, Hezekiah. According to scriptures, when he became king over Israel, "he did that which was evil in the sight of God".

In fact, he engaged in all sorts of evils, including idolatry, which God detest very much. Yet when he repented, God gave him a second chance and turned his destiny around for the better. Do you desire a second chance from the almighty; receive it now in the name of Jesus. Amen! Beloved, have you lived a riotous and wicked life in the past, are your sins so bad that you are afraid that God may not forgive you?

Saint! I prophesy God shall hear your supplication if you would repent now, turn away from your evil ways and turn towards the Lord. I assure you, God will turn your destiny around! He did it for Manasseh; He did it for Rahab the harlot. He will do even more for you. He is ready and willing to restore you unto Himself. The choice is yours. Be ye transformed by repenting, return to God by the renewal of your mind and God will return to you and bless you. Amen!

Prayer: Lord Hear and answer my petitions in Jesus' name!

May 12th

[ONE YEAR BIBLE PLAN: 2 Kings 15-16/ John 3:1-18]

Today's Word: Hebrews 11:6

"But without faith it is impossible to please Him, for he who comes to God must believe that He is, and that He is a rewarder of those who diligently seek Him."

MY FAITH WILL SHOW IN MY FAITHFULNESS!

Many people are in a dilemma when it comes to differentiating between faith and faithfulness. They faithfully serve God, but as they go through hardship in life, they begin to wonder why God won't respond to them even though they serve God faithfully. Why wouldn't He just do this or do that for them? This has led to bitterness in many people's lives. Faithfulness is one of the most important virtues every child of God must exhibit. God will surely bless you for your faithfulness. The more faithful you are, the greater the level of responsibilities that are committed to you! [Luke 16:10].

But as wonderful as faithfulness is, it won't change a thing in your life. It won't bring the money you need, or get you healed. It takes faith to change hopeless and challenging situations not faithfulness. Faith is the victory that overcomes the world not faithfulness. [1 John 5:4]. Poverty, afflictions and infirmities will only respond to faith not faithfulness. It is your faith in God's Word that will change things for good for you. If you've been feeling that God has neglected you in spite of your faithfulness, then you've confused faith with faithfulness. You must build your faith strong with the Word of God, and you will be able to face any crisis and win!

Prayer: I will not confuse faith with faithfulness*!*

May 13th

[ONE YEAR BIBLE PLAN: 2 Kings 17-18/ John 3:19-36]

Today's Word: Psalm 69:14

"Deliver me out of the mire, and let me not sink; let me be delivered from those who hate me, and out of the deep waters."

GOD SHALL DELIVER ME FROM HATERS!

The declaration above is very important in the life of a person who is hated because the force of hate is very destructive. It can make even those that are supposed to be close to you to harm you. Joseph never imagined that his brothers [whom he loved and cared so much for; as to search them out in the forest] could conspire to kill or sell him into slavery in a strange land. But that is what hatred does. [Genesis 37]

Sometimes people hate others for no obvious fault or reason. For Joseph; the mere fact that he narrated his God-given dreams to his brothers generated so much hate that his own blood brothers were ready to kill him. However, because God cared for him, he was delivered from the hands of the haters.

I don't know how many people hate your guts because of your God-given abilities. Maybe like Joseph, your kith and kin have conspired against you. Or maybe you are afraid to go to your workplace because it seems like your colleagues are always finding one reason or the other to antagonize you.

This day as the Oracle of God, I decree that the Lord God shall deliver you from all your haters in the name of Jesus. Amen!

Prayer: Father! Deliver me from all my haters in the name of Jesus Christ. Amen!

May 14th

[ONE YEAR BIBLE PLAN: 2 Kings 19-21/ John 4:1-30]

The Word Today: Ezra 9:8

*"And now for a little while grace has been shown from the Lord our God, to leave us a **remnant** to escape, and to give us a peg in His holy place, that our God may enlighten our eyes and give us a measure of revival in our bondage."*

REMNANT [HEBREW] 'SHA'AR'

'Sha'ar' is the Hebrew for 'remnant' as used in our text-verse above and also in 'Ezra 9:15' Strong's Concordance #7604: To be a remnant means 'to remain' or 'to be left over'. A remnant is what survives after a catastrophe. In Ezra, the word frequently refers to those Israelites who survived the Exile and returned to resettle in the Promised Land [Ezra 9:8].

The prophets use the word to speak not only of a group of Israelites who survived a particular calamity; but to those Israelites who remained faithful to God [Amos 5:14-15].

The concept of the remnant is central to Isaiah, who prophesies that the root of Jesse, the Messiah, would one day gather the remnant of Israel from all nations, even attracting many Gentiles to Himself [Isaiah 11:10-11, Isaiah 11:16].

The remnant therefore becomes a powerful Old Testament theme of covenant faithfulness and salvation, for in sparing His people; God maintained a nation through who the whole world would be blessed [Genesis 12:3].

Third Sunday of the Month of May

[ONE YEAR BIBLE PLAN: 2 Kings 22-23/ John 4:31-54]

CHURCH AND HOME SUNDAY SCHOOL

What does the bible teach about the laying on of hands for receiving the Holy Spirit?

The gift of the Holy Spirit can also be impacted by the laying on of hands.

1. The believers at Samaria received the Holy Spirit by the laying on of hands. Acts 8:18-19 *"And when Simon saw that through the laying on of the apostles' hands the Holy Spirit was given, he offered them money, saying, "Give me this power also, that anyone on whom I lay hands may receive the Holy Spirit."*

2. Paul the Apostle received the Holy Spirit by the laying on of hands. Acts 9:17 *"And Ananias went his way and entered the house; and laying his hands on him he said, "Brother Saul, the Lord Jesus, who appeared to you on the road as you came, has sent me that you may receive your sight and be filled with the Holy Spirit."*

3. Believers at Ephesus received the Holy Spirit by the laying on of hands. Acts 19:6 *"And when Paul had laid hands on them, the Holy Spirit came upon them, and they spoke with tongues and prophesied."*

Sunday School Question

1) What does the bible teach about laying on of hands for receiving the holy spirit?

Memory Verse: Acts 19:6 "And when Paul had laid hands on them, the Holy Spirit came upon them, and they spoke with tongues and prophesied."

May 16th

[ONE YEAR BIBLE PLAN: 2 Kings 24-25/ John 5:1-24]

Today's Word: Psalm 120:1-3

I AM DELIVERED FROM DECEITFUL PEOPLE!

As you make good plans and work hard to achieving your goals, there is the need to pray for divine protection and preservations from those whose, threefold demonic ministry is to kill, to steal and to destroy. Experience has shown and proven that deception, conspiracy and intrigue is the greatest wile of the devil.

In counseling sessions, I have encountered so many people who refuse to aspire for greater height because of what deceitful friends and relatives have done to them in the past. Many become very suspicious and afraid to venture into anything at all or deal with anyone. Some are so cautious that they refuse to divulge certain information because of past ugly experience with men and women of God wherein they were exploited.

Such is the level of trickery and deceit perpetuated by the devil and his cohort in the world. The after effect is total loss of confidence in humanity resulting in the inability to achieve anything in life. Are you experiencing such situation? If so, know that; not every human being is evil. There are many good people out there too, as there are bad ones. The earlier you let go of your unpleasant past, the better for you. Pray now this prayer to free your spirit!

Prayer: Lord! Place a right spirit within me in Jesus' name. Amen!

May 17th

[ONE YEAR BIBLE PLAN: 1 Chronicles 1-3/ John 5:25-47]

Today's Word: 2 Kings 20:12-18

I WILL NOT FALL PREY TO THE WILES OF MY ENEMIES!

When Jeremiah, in Jeremiah 17:9 said the heart of a man *"deceitful above all things and desperately wicked..."* He sure knew what he was saying. Surely, man's heart is hideous and can't be deciphered except by God. How in the world could King Hezekiah have known that the emissaries sent to him by the king of Babylon with a goodwill message were actually spies that came to learn his secrets? Unaware of their real intentions, Hezekiah showed them all the secrets of his kingdom including his wealthy, treasure and his military might. Babylon later used the information to conquer Judah and carted away many captives during Daniels captivity.

This strategy is still being used today by the kingdom of darkness and wickedness to wreck havoc in the lives of God's people. Your unfriendly friends would ask about your plans and progress but with dubious intentions. Many close to you, pretending to be well-wishers are actually seeking your downfall. That is why you must guard your plans and ideas jealously. You must be wise in dealing with people of the world. Do you have plans? Are you expecting a breakthrough? Wait until the result is made manifest before you begin to broadcast it. Remember your enemies can also be members of your household. And I decree you will not fall prey to the wiles of Satan in Jesus mighty name. Amen!

Prayer! I declare I will not fall victim to the wiles of the devil!

May 18th

[ONE YEAR BIBLE PLAN: 1 Chronicles 4-6/ John 6:1-21]

Today's Word: Hebrews 11:1

MY FAITH WILL ESTABLISH MY HOPE!

"Faith is the substance of things hoped for..." and therein lies the difference between hope and faith. Faith has substance, and proof that what you hoped for has become yours, but hope has no substance! Hope is futuristic; but faith is now! Hope is looking forward to or looking over a wall at something you desire for, praying that one day it will become yours. But faith is you climbing that wall and taking hold of that which you hope for or grabbing the necessary document or title deeds to take ownership of that which you hope for or desire. So, while hope says *"I am going to have it..."* Faith says *"I have it now!"* The bible says the just shall live by faith not by hope! [Hebrews 10:38]. As far as faith is concern, whatever you hope for; you already have and you must act like it. I don't mean you should pretend that you have it but declare it into manifestation; seeing that you already have it in the spirit. Unlike hope, faith does not wait for God, when God is waiting for you to use your faith to usher in what He has already accomplished.

Faith says thank You Lord, for You have made all things ready for me and given me all that I require for life and godliness. I claim every blessing therein in Your Word. While hope puts thing in perspective and 'sweet by and by', faith takes possession now. It is faith that catapults you into your inheritance in Christ not hope! For you to reign in life, your hope must be converted to faith by accepting what God has said, and speaking it into your life, in spite of contrary circumstances and surrounding situations.

May 19th

[ONE YEAR BIBLE PLAN: 1 Chronicles 7-9/ John 6:22-44]

Today's Word: Mark 11:12-26

I DECREE! THE MOUNTAINS BEFORE ME ARE CAST INTO THE DEEP BLUE SEA!

In our text-passage above, Jesus Christ was teaching mankind a very important principle; the most effective way to solve problems. A mountain represents stubborn obstacles and problems that impede human progress in life.

When Jesus was talking to the tree in verse 14, the disciples must have wondered what was wrong with Him. They could not have imagined that the tree was hearing and would eventually obey Him. But the next day when it dawned on them that the tree had obeyed, they understood what He was teaching them. When God speaks everything hears. Just as that tree heard and obeyed Jesus in our text passage above, so also will your problems hear and obey you as you speak in faith to them in Jesus name. If only you can have strong faith you will definitely have cause to glorify God always in your testimonies in Jesus' name. Amen!

Are there obstacles that refused to allow you make progress in life? I admonish you now arise and begin to speak to them in faith; command them to be cast into the deep blue sea. As you do so, I join my faith with yours and I decree that those mountains of issues in your life be remove and cast into the deep blue sea in the name of Jesus. Amen!

Prayer: Your Mountains of issues in my life be cast into the deep blue sea in Jesus' mighty name. Amen!

May 20th

[ONE YEAR BIBLE PLAN: 1 Chron. 10-12/ John 6:45-71]

Today's Word: Psalm 50:14-15

GOD WILL ANSWER ME AS I FULFILL MY VOW!

The most important thing about vow that you should note in [Psalm 50:14-15] is that; if you call on God in the day of trouble He will surely answer you and He will deliver you and you shall glorify Him. But in [verse 14] you will see the condition on which the verse is operative. Psalm 50:14 says *"Offer unto God thanksgiving and pay thy vows unto the most high and call upon me in the day of trouble, I will deliver thee and thou shalt glorify me".* Now if you don't speed-read the Bible, if you read the scriptures carefully, you will observe that, at the end of [verse 14] there is no full stop. [No period]. The point here is that, the story continues onto [verse 15]. It said you must do two things: One, offer unto God, thanksgiving: I pray God give you the grace to be appreciative in Jesus' name! And number two pay your vows unto the Most High and then call on the Lord in the day of trouble. He will surely deliver you and you will glorify Him. I admonish you right now to make a vow.

I have made several vows before and I can tell you one thing, God has never failed on His Word. I want you to bow your heads for a few minutes and challenge the Almighty! Say, "Father do this for me and I will do that for you." Talk to Him for a while; just tell Him, Father, I know that You are the Almighty, I know You are the covenant keeping God, there is nothing You can't do. Do this for me and I will do that for You in Jesus' name. Amen!

Prayer: Father! Answer me speedily in Jesus' name. Amen!

May 21st

[ONE YEAR BIBLE PLAN: 1 Chron. 13-15/ John 7:1-27]

WORD SWORD OF THE ORACLE

Today's Word: Nehemiah 1:6

"please let Your ear be attentive and Your eyes open, that You may hear the prayer of Your servant which I pray before You now, day and night, for the children of Israel Your servants, and confess the sins of the children of Israel which we have sinned against You. Both my father's house and I have sinned."

CONFESS [HEBREW] 'YADAH'

'Yadah' is the Hebrew word for 'confess' as used in the above scripture and also in [Leviticus 5:5; Numbers 5:7; Psalm 92:1; Psalm 106:47] Strong's Concordance #3034:

This Hebrew verb conveys two distinct meanings. The first is related to the offering of thanksgiving or praise to God [2 Chronicles 5:13; Psalm 92:1; Psalm 106:47].

The second is that of confession, such as the confession of God's greatness [1 Kings 8:33; 1 Kings 8:35] and confession of sin before God [Nehemiah 1:6; Nehemiah 9:2; Daniel 9:4].

The basic meaning of the word 'Yadah' is "to throw" or "to cast off." In one sense, confession is the "casting off" of sin by acknowledging our transgressions of God's commandments for holy living [Psalm 32:5; Proverbs 28:13]. In another sense, confession of sin is thanksgiving because it recognizes that forgiveness of sin is accomplished only by grace and by the goodness of God [2 Chronicles 30:22; Daniel 9:4].

Fourth Sunday of the Month of May

[ONE YEAR BIBLE PLAN: 1 Chron. 16-18/ John 7:28-53]

CHURCH AND HOME SUNDAY SCHOOL

What does the bible teach about the laying on of hands for confirmations?

Confirmation through laying-on of hands is the means whereby members of the church are settled, strengthened and established in the faith of Jesus Christ. This is for the believers who have been taught the doctrines, ordinances and sacraments of the church and have experienced them. Acts 15:32 *"Now Judas and Silas, themselves being prophets also, exhorted and strengthened the brethren with many words."*

WHAT DOES THE BIBLE TEACH ABOUT THE LAYING ON OF HANDS FOR ORDINATION?

Ordination is conferred upon those entering full time ministry, to vest them with ministerial functions and authority by laying-on of hands. Acts 13:1-3 *"....ministered to the Lord and fasted, the Holy Spirit said, "Now separate to Me Barnabas and Saul for the work to which I have called them." Then, having fasted and prayed and laid hands on them, they sent them away."*

Sunday School Question

1) What does the bible teach about the laying on of hands for confirmations?
2) What does the bible teach about the laying on hands for ordination?

Memory Verse: Acts 13:3 "Then, having fasted and prayed and laid hands on them, they sent them away."

May 23rd

[ONE YEAR BIBLE PLAN: 1 Chron. 19-21/ John 8:1-27]

Today's Word: Luke 17:11-19; Psalm 95:2

I DECREE! UPON MY LIFE THE BLESSINGS OF GRATITUDE!

God lavishes blessings upon us daily. And, just like natural parent, He expects us to appreciate His goodness and mercies. But today, many take God's blessings for granted. We assume that when we sleep, we must wake up, or when we are sick, we shall be healed. We feel God is obligated to shelter us from all attacks of our enemies. We assume that God will continue to be nice to us no matter what! If you are like that; how wrong you are; you are dead wrong!

From our text- passage above; we see that God expects us to show appreciation for each blessing. Jesus asked: *'Were not ten cleansed? Where are the other nine?'* In any area you've failed to appreciate God, you become a debtor therein. Pay your thanksgiving debts today so that it does not count against you later. Appreciating God entails testifying boldly to God's glory for what He has done; worshipping in total surrender to His will; and thanking Him from the bottom of your heart. Through thanksgiving, your blessings are made permanent and you can experience complete restoration. Be sure to live a daily life of gratitude to God. Begin now to thank God for past mercies and blessings, itemizing them one by one. Count your blessings one by one and you will see clearly how much more He will do for you. Alleluia!

Prayer: Lord! Today I thank You for Your past and present mercies and goodness in Jesus' name. Amen!

May 24th

[ONE YEAR BIBLE PLAN: 1 Chron. 22-24/ John 8:28-59]

Today's Word: Exodus 18:13-27

GOD WILL SEND WISE COUNSELORS TO GUIDE ME!

The outcome of your life is to a large extent dependant on the type of counsel you receive. If you receive and act on foolish counsel you eventually end up a failure in life. But you become successful if you receive and act on good and wise counsel. No one is different from the counsel available to him/her. That is why [Psalm 1:1-3] say one should avoid ungodly counsel. But for Jethro, Moses would've most likely died an untimely death because of the workload on him. Moses obedience to the voice of good and wise counsel from Jethro ensured that he achieved more result with less effort and lived longer.

What kind of counsel are you exposed to? Do you still hang out in clubs with night crawlers? Do you always spend time with unsuccessful people? One way or the other, the people you hang out with will soon begin to influence the outcome of your life. The longer you are with them the faster you imbibe their characteristics. [Amos 3:3] That is why after a long time in marriage spouse begin to think alike, act alike and even look alike. Do you aspire for success in life? Seek wise counsel and act on them accordingly and I declare the Lord God will send wise counselors to guide you to good success in the name of Jesus Christ. Amen! Remain Blessed!

Prayer: Lord Jesus! Grant me the grace to receive and act on good and wise counsel to guide me to good success!

May 25th

[ONE YEAR BIBLE PLAN: 1 Chron. 25-27/ John 9:1-23]

Today's Word: Zechariah 4:8-10

I DECREE! MY HANDS WILL COMPLETE ALL THAT I STARTED!

Months ago a young couple called for prayer and counseling. According to them, they had helped several people transact business only to be short-changed at the last minute. They had worked very hard to start several projects in their work place, only to be taken away from them as soon as there are signs of progress and success.

I cited and referred them to certain scriptures like our text passage above; from which I made them understand that they were actually operating under a curse. Consequently, by the knowledge, I placed them on fasting and prayers and the curse was broken by the shed blood of Jesus Christ [Galatians 3:13-14]. And since then things have turned out better for them.

In our text-passage the Israelites were under the curse of wastage and abandoned projects. They were laboring in vain without any visible gain and the Lord stepped in and broke the curse that was upon Zerubbabel. Accordingly, the glory of God changed his sad story to a glorious one; and he became a cornerstone for God.

Are you under a curse? Are you always starting well but finishing badly or not finishing at all? I decree the curse broken now in the name of Jesus Christ. Amen!

Prayer: I decree every curse in my life broken in Jesus' name!

May 26th

[ONE YEAR BIBLE PLAN: 1 Chron. 28-29/ John 9:24-41]

Today's Word: Psalm 9:14-16

ANY TRAP SET FOR ME SHALL ENSARE THE SETTER!

"*I* got wedded in 1990, to a man who claimed to be a mechanical engineer but after the marriage, I discovered he was an occultist. Soon enough strife began as I opted to get out of the marriage. Within six months we were divorced, in anger my ex-husband cast a spell on me and for the following twenty-one years, I was afflicted with all manner of diseases that defied modern medicine. I went from hospital to hospital, from lab to lab. Test upon test upon test. I went from one prayer house to another, one church to another in desperation seeking cure to no avail. Then I learnt of The Oracle of God PRAYER CONFERENCE LINE and came on: Pastor Stevie prayed for me and placed me on a seven day fast. On the fifth day I became whole again. And I called the man of God and told him I am well now can I stop the fasting, because I have never previously fasted beyond three days, he prayed and said if I want to know who was responsible for my ordeal I should continue with the fast and that the person will not only confess but he will carry his evil load and in ninety days I will be married. So I continued with the fast. On the seventh day of my fast, my ex- confessed that he was responsible for my affliction and few days later he became afflicted with every ailment I went through. I give God all the glory for saving me! Now I am married and expecting a set of twins a boy and a girl glory to God! Sister XXXX.

Prayer: Arrow of affliction fired into my life backfire now!

May 27th

[ONE YEAR BIBLE PLAN: 2 Chronicles 1-3/ John 10:1-23]

Today's Word: 2 Kings 2:1-9

I DECREE! I SHALL NOT BE DISTRACTED FROM MY BREAKTHROUGH!

From every indication, focused people always succeed in life. They are not distracted by side attractions. Elisha was of such stock. As soon as he made up his mind on what he wanted, he refused to accept any other thing but success. Otherwise, the mockery of the other sons of the prophet' was enough to discourage him and make him end his pursuit. But the more they jeered at him the more resolute he became to achieve result. In fact, his firm resolve was proven by the fact that not even Elijah's counsel that he should go back; stopped him. Instead he used every discouraging situation to encourage himself. Surely such behavior is worthy of emulation.

What is it you are seeking from God? I decree receive it now in Jesus' name! Everyone on a great assignment in life faces one distraction or the other. It could come from people around you or situations around you. But the level of your success depends on your response to such distractions. Those who allow themselves to be weighed down eventually lose out on their goals; while those who ignore the distractions eventually achieve success. Are you facing one form of distraction or the other? I admonish you to remain focused and you shall not be distracted from your breakthrough in Jesus' name. Amen!

Prayer: I commit myself to achieving every noble desire of my heart without wavering. I refuse to be confused or distracted!

May 28th

[ONE YEAR BIBLE PLAN: 2 Chron. 4-6/ John 10:24-42]

WORD SWORD OF THE ORACLE

Today's Word: Nehemiah 3:20

"After him Baruch the son of Zabbai carefully repaired the other section, from the buttress to the door of the house of Eliashib the high priest."

CAREFULLY [HEBREW] 'CHARAH'

The Hebrew word for 'carefully' is 'Charah' as used in our text-verse above and also in [Exodus 32:10; Jonah 4:1] Strong's Concordance #2734:

Strange as it may sound, the Hebrew verb translated carefully here usually means "to burn with anger" [Genesis 39:19, Jonah 4:1] and it also depicts anger as a burning fire. This is the type of intense anger or wrath displayed by the Lord God when the children of Israel worshiped a worthless idol of a golden calf instead of their Deliverer; in the wilderness when Moses went for the Ten Commandment and took too long to return [Exodus 32:10]. In this passage the word is translated "burn hot"

In our text-passage above, the word denotes 'burning zeal', not wrath or anger. In other words, Baruch earnestly wanted the walls of Jerusalem repaired or rebuilt because he knew it was God's city, and God's work. His repair works were for the glory of the living God and not for his own personal glory.

Prayer: Father turn your wrath and anger away from me in Jesus' name. Amen!

Fifth Sunday of the Month of May

[ONE YEAR BIBLE PLAN: 2 Chronicles 7-9/ John 11:1-29]

CHURCH AND HOME SUNDAY SCHOOL

What does the bible teaches about the laying on of hands with prophecy?

When believers are ready to begin a ministry or train for a ministry in the church, there can be an impartation of the creative Spirit of God by laying-on of hands. Spiritual gifts and ministries are spoken into being by the anointed word of prophecy. 1 Timothy 4:14 *"Do not neglect the gift that is in you, which was given to you by prophecy with the laying on of the hands of the eldership."*

1 Timothy 1:18 *"This charge I commit to you, son Timothy, according to the prophecies previously made concerning you, that by them you may wage the good warfare."*

1 Thessalonians 5:19 *"Do not quench the Spirit."*

WHAT BENEFIT DOES THIS DOCTRINE OF LAYING-ON OF HANDS IMPART ON US? Through the doctrine of the laying-on of hands and by faith; we can also be a channel of blessing to others.

Sunday school question

1) What does the bible teaches about the laying on of hands with prophecy?
2) What benefit does this doctrine of laying-on of hands impart on us?

Memory Verse: 1Timothy 1:18 *"This charge I commit to you, son ..., according to the prophecies ... made concerning you, that... you may wage the good warfare."*

May 30th

[ONE YEAR BIBLE PLAN: 2 Chron. 10-12/ John 11:30-57]

Today's Word: Matthew 8:23-27

I DECREE! CALM UNTO ALL MY LIFE'S CRISIS!

The above tempest story; true as it is, it is also a metaphor, telling us not to be moved by circumstance around us. It is also very instructive to note that Jesus is asleep in a destructive tempest that was tossing the ship around. Even more educative is, the reaction of Jesus when He woke up. Instead of jumping up frantically, to assess and assist in the situation, he calmly said *"why are ye fearful, O ye of little faith?"*

Saint, are you frightened because you are in one crisis or the other? Is it your investment that is in limbo? Are you scared of getting into a new venture due to past failures? Is it your present health? Beloveth, Christ is asking you now the same question that; He ask His disciples two thousand years ago *"why are ye fearful, O ye of little faith?"* He wants you to know that you are the master of your destiny, that no crisis, issues, problems or obstacles around about you should be able to shape your destiny, if you don't allow it. You may not be able to decide which obstacle will come your way, but you should decide which battle to fight and win. You must choose how to react to your issues in fear or in faith; the choice is yours. And your reaction will determine the outcome of your trials. Beloveth just focus on Jesus when faced with crisis and difficulties and you will prevail in Jesus' name. Amen!

Prayer: Every crisis in my life both physical and spiritual be still now in Jesus' name. Amen!

May 31st

[ONE YEAR BIBLE PLAN: 2 Chron. 13-14/ John 12:1-26]

Today's Word: Jeremiah 30:14-17

GOD WILL HEAL ME OF ALL MY HURTS!

Is your life a story of agony, and sorrow? Has your loved ones abandoned and forsaken you? Are your woes compounded because you forsook the Lord your God?

Saint! I bring you good tidings from the throne of grace this day! I decree! The Lord shall heal you of your wounds in Jesus' name. Amen!

Today marks the end of your sufferings. The sovereign God of Israel has decided to have mercy on you [Romans 9:15]. This means from this day, your sorrowful tears are over with.

A smile is about to appear on your face for it is written: *"I will restore health unto thee, and I will heal thee of thy wounds."* God is also promising to restore everything you have lost during your years of toiling and suffering in the name of Jesus Christ. Amen! [Joel 2:25-26].

In addition, He promised to devour all those who have devoured you, He would spoil those who spoiled you and prey on those that preyed upon you in your days of pain. So, cheer up for surely there is an end, and this day mark the end of your anguish, and signals the beginning of a brand new day for you and your family in Jesus' name. Amen!

Prayer: Lord Jesus! Blot out every source of pain in my life in Jesus' name. Amen!

June 01

[ONE YEAR BIBLE PLAN: 2 Chron. 15-16/ John 12:27-50]

Today's Word: Hebrews 13:15

I RECEIVE GOD'S FAITHFULNESS AS I PRAISE HIM!

Most people leave praising God behind as they leave the Church building. You ought not to take praising God for an event that happens only when you gather together with other saints in the church. Praise should be your lifestyle as a believer; it ought to be part and parcel of your daily prayer life. At your daily devotionals, at work, in the car, at home in bed, or anywhere, everywhere and every time. Continually praising God brings the supernatural to play in your life. Praise God extraordinarily now!

Father You are worthy of my praises today. Eternal rock of ages I bless Your Holy name. You are the Highest. You are the Greatest, You are the Best. The Oldest, The Wisest! You are the Richest. You are the Prince of peace, Immortal God. Invincible, the Only Wise God, the Alpha, and the Omega, the Beginning, and the Ending, Counselor, mighty God, the Everlasting Father, glory be to Your holy name in Jesus' name I worship. Amen!

PRAYER FOR JUNE BIRTHDAY!

Father! Thank You for Your children, born in June and those celebrating any anniversary this month: June is the 6th month of the year; and six is five plus one. That is grace plus extra one. Lord, in their lives, grant them extra miracles, extra blessings, extra joy, extra promotions, extra progress; in their marriages extra bliss and blessings in Jesus' name. Amen!

June 02

[ONE YEAR BIBLE PLAN: 2 Chron. 17-18/ John 13:1-20]

Today's Word: Numbers 11:1-10

LUST OF THE FLESH WILL NOT DESTROY ME!

If there is one thing God hates; it is succumbing to the lust or desire of the flesh by Believers. That is what caused the death of many Israelites in the desert. Even though they had been delivered from Egypt; they still craved Egypt in the sin of gluttony.

Consequently, they complained severally for lack of garlic and spicy food. This so angered God that Moses had to intercede; for them not be destroyed in the wilderness instantly. Their behavior can be compared to those who look back on their days in sin with nostalgia. They grumble albeit silently at the restrictions of the Christian life. This makes many professing Christians fall back into sin.

Are you one of such Believer? If you are, I tell you the truth, you are still in Egypt; bound with the sin of the lust of flesh. You are like the children of Israel who craved the onions and garlic of captivity rather than the things of the Lord [Manna].

I decree that the lust and desires of flesh will not derail your destiny in Jesus' name. Like Moses interceded for Israel; I stand in the gap for you now, I decree the destruction of the yoke of seductive and addictive sin in your life in Jesus' name. Amen!

Prayer: Every craving and desire of the flesh in my life is crushed now by the anointed Blood of Jesus Christ!

June 03rd

[ONE YEAR BIBLE PLAN: 2 Chron. 19-20/ John 13:21-38]

Today's Word: 2 Kings 2:9-15

I AM READY FOR MY BREAKTHROUGH!

I read and re-read the story of Elijah and Elisha severally, without fully understanding the enormity of Elijah's charge to Elisha until the Holy Spirit of God enlightened me. Many would argue that what Elijah told Elisha, his protégé to do was not a difficult task, but a critical analysis of the charge proves otherwise. Agreeing to fulfill Elijah's condition meant a lot of responsibility for Elisha. The implication is that he had to be vigilant and keep Elijah within his view 24/7. It meant he could neither sleep nor rest wholesomely until the translation of Elijah. It meant that as long as Elijah remained with him, Elisha could not focus on any other thing but his master. What a task?

Is that not a difficult condition? Surely it is! Many people are unable to secure their miracles because of lack of focus. They pray and fast for breakthrough, they wait patiently for it to happen. But, sometimes in a momentary lack of concentration, they lose the manifestation of their testimonies to distractions. Such people need to pray for alertness of mind and of the spirit to encounter divine intervention. Are you one of such people? If so, I hereby release heavenly alertness upon your spirit-man now. And I prophesy... you shall be ready when your miracle comes in Jesus' name. Amen!

Prayer: I receive grace to wait for my miracle and I shall be ready when it comes in Jesus' name. Amen!

June 04th

[ONE YEAR BIBLE PLAN: 2 Chronicles 21-22/ John 14]

WORD SWORD OF THE ORACLE

Today's Word: Nehemiah 1:5

*"And I said: "I pray, Lord God of heaven, O great and **awesome** God, You who keep Your covenant and mercy with those who love You and observe Your commandments."*

AWESOME [HEBREW] YARE'

The word 'awesome' in Hebrew is the word Yare' as used in our text-verse above and also as in [Nehemiah 4:4; Genesis 32:11] Strong's Concordance #3372:

This Hebrew word translated 'awesome' is derived from the Hebrew verb meaning "to fear". In this context, the word does not suggest or does not mean "frightened." Rather it suggests the quality that inspires reverence or godly fear.

In some scriptural passages, in the bible, "fearing" and godly living are so closely related that they are almost synonymous [Leviticus 19:14; Leviticus 25:17; Deuteronomy 17:19; 2 Kings 17:34].

Thus while ordinary fear paralyzes a person, godly fear leads to submission and obedience to the Lord God Almighty. The person who properly fears God avoids evil [Job 1:1] and walks in God's ways Psalm: 128:1 *"Blessed is everyone who fears the Lord, Who walks in His ways."*

Prayer: Awesome God! Bring Your fear upon me so as to avoid sin in the name of Jesus. Amen!

First Sunday of the Month of June

[ONE YEAR BIBLE PLAN: [2 Chronicles 23-24/ John 15]

CHURCH AND HOME SUNDAY SCHOOL

THE PURPOSE OF THE NEW COVENANT!

What is the purpose of the new covenant?

The purpose of the New Covenant is to prepare us for the second coming of Jesus Christ to earth.

Acts 1:10-11 *"And while they looked steadfastly toward heaven as He went up, behold, two men stood by them in white apparel, who also said, "Men of Galilee, why do you stand gazing up into heaven? This same Jesus, who was taken up from you into heaven, will so come in like manner as you saw Him go into heaven."*

WHAT IS THE DOCTRINE OF RESURRECTION OF THE DEAD?

It is the belief that God will raise the dead to life again.

John 11:25 *"Jesus said to her, "I am the resurrection and the life. He who believes in Me, though he may die, he shall live."*

Sunday school question

1) What is the purpose of the new covenant?
2) What is the doctrine of resurrection of the dead?

Memory Verse: John 11:25 "Jesus said to her, "I am the resurrection and the life. He who believes in Me, though he may die, he shall live."

June 06th

[ONE YEAR BIBLE PLAN: 2 Chronicles 24-27/ John 16]

Today's Word: Hebrews 11:1

I DECLARE! I SHALL PUT MY FAITH TO WORK!

Faith is the substance of things hope for, the evidence of unseen realities. Faith possesses in the present what you hope for. Walking in this realm is bringing to play the demonstration of faith. For instant, you might have prayed for something concerning yourself, believing God will do it. If you truly believe that God heard your prayer, then you shouldn't come back and pray for the same thing. You should only begin to thank Him for it; you begin to act like you already received your petition from God: that's how to put your faith to work effectively.

Faith is active and not passive. Faith acts now because it takes possession now. This is what [James 2:17] is saying: faith without action is dead; it doesn't work. The faith that works; is faith with work: i.e. faith that acts on the believed Word of God.

So, if you truly believe God's Word; and believe that He is who He say He is; and will do what He says He will do; and has done what He says He has done; and believe that you have what He says you have; then you must talk, walk, act and live that way. Therefore when you pray, act as someone that have received what he/she believes; that's how to put your faith to work. And I decree from henceforth, your faith will work for you as you put it to work in Jesus' name. Amen!

Prayer: Lord! Help me put my faith to work in Jesus' name!

June 07th

[ONE YEAR BIBLE PLAN: 2 Chronicles 28-29/ John 17]

Today's Word: Genesis 17:15-19; Genesis 21:1-3

I DECLARE! GOD'S BLESSINGS UPON ME SHALL CONFOUND ME!

Scientifically and humanly speaking, menopause is the age at which a woman can no longer conceive and this occurs between the ages of forty-five and fifty-five. Sarah, Abraham' wife had doubled that age as at the time God was still declaring the promise of Isaac to her. Not only that, even Abraham' body would have stopped producing reproductive seed.

By all physical and medical standards, the couple was not in any position to procreate. That is why Abraham asked God to bless Ishmael whom he already had. But God is not a man! And His ways are not the ways of men! When He says He would do a thing, then nothing can stop Him. So, in order to prove to Abraham in particular and to mankind in general; that He created all things; He recreated the couple's reproductive system so that they bore Isaac! Glory to God!

Saint! Are you expecting some miracles from God? Have you waited too long that you now think that God has forgotten you? Or like Abraham, are you now searching for alternatives? Today, as the Oracle of God, I decree that the blessings of the God of Abraham are released upon you now in the name of Jesus. God will so bless you that you shall be confounded in the name of Jesus. Amen!

Prayer: I command my blessings released now in Jesus' name!

June 08th

[ONE YEAR BIBLE PLAN: 2 Chron. 30-31/ John 18:1-18]

Today's Word: Matthew 9:19-22

THE LORD HAS MADE ME WHOLE!

"What you think you saw is not what you really saw." It is common knowledge that humans have one issue or the other bothering them at various points in their lives. Many people's problems may not be obvious: there is more to them than meet the eyes. 'There is An African adage that says all lizards lay prostrated; so no one can tell which one has stomach ache'. So, except a person tells you of his or her problem you may not know about it. For some people, their problems are financial challenges; for others it may be health issues; for some, marital settlement or inability to procreate. In ministry, I have come across all kinds of issues of life. In fact, I have seen and heard so much to know that everyone needs to be made whole. I don't know what your area of need is; but I do know that there is someone who can meet all your needs. And that person is Jesus Christ; He does deed to meet every need. By the power that is in His name and His blood, I prophesy, you are made whole now. The woman with the issue of blood in [Matthew 9:19-22] needed to be made whole. For twelve whole years she bled excessively nonstop. And, had become hopeless; she must have been waiting to die but then she heard Jesus was in town, and hope returned to her. She decision to receive her healing by touching the garment of Jesus and she got it immediately. I decree, according to your faith so shall it be unto you in the name of Jesus. Amen!

Prayer: Lord! Make whole again in Jesus' name. Amen!

June 09th

[ONE YEAR BIBLE PLAN: [2 Chron. 32-33/ John 18:19-40]

Today's Word: Exodus 23:20-23

"Behold, I send an Angel before you to keep you in the way and to bring you into the place which I have prepared......"

THE LORD GOD SHALL GO AHEAD OF ME!

Throughout the annals of Christianity, records show that those who achieved great successes with God were people who had the presence of God with them. From Abraham to Isaac, Jacob, Joseph to Moses, Gideon, Jephthah etc; they all achieved great works by God's help and divine presence.

When God goes before you, your assignment is made easy. Because God is all-knowing, He knows the end from the beginning. So, if you engage Him in your affairs; your circumstances would be rearranged in your favor from the very onset. That is why the Israelites overcame all their enemies on the way to the Land of Promise. In the text above, God reiterated the importance of divine presence in our lives. He said; as long as His angel is with us, no evil will befall us. And in spite of all the obstacles to our miracles, we would reach our desire goals in Jesus' mighty name. Amen!

Saint! Whatever goal you have set out to achieve this month, this year, and in life; I decree you shall testify in the name of Jesus! You shall no longer toil in vain without gain! God shall prosper the works of your hands; no adversaries shall stop you from the glory that God has for you in Jesus' name. Amen!

Prayer: Lord! Lead me through the path of life to a successful destiny in the name of Jesus Christ. Amen!

June 10th

[ONE YEAR BIBLE PLAN: 2 Chron. 34-36/ John 19:1-22]

Today's Word: John 6:1-3

MY MOUTH WILL MAKE PEOPLE SEEK ME!

Jesus had a humbled up-bringing: the father was a carpenter; the mother Mary, a simple housewife. Jesus' background was not in any peculiar way inspiring. So, He was not accepted in Nazareth during the early years of His ministry. But in the process of time, His story became a story of crowds and multitudes besieging Him, seeking Him out everywhere He went. They sought after him because of His value; His worth. When people come around Jesus, all kind of things happens; the sick get their healing, the lame walk, the blind see, the dumb spoke and the needy receive provisions. Jesus just kept adding value to peoples' life. He was a solution to peoples' problem; so He was never alone. What is your life like? Do you always seek position in order to impart other people's life positively? Or do you feel irrelevant in society because of your poor background? Jesus never worked as a high level diplomat nor was He from a wealthy family. Yet He was sought after more than any other person with such privileges. Jesus was sought after because He added value to the society and to peoples' life. I don't know what you do, but I do know that, if you can make yourself a solution provider, men and women from all works of life will sought after you. Tell people about Jesus, counsel and pray for people always. And as you do so, men will seek you to bless you because of your value and you shall be great in Jesus' name. Amen!

Prayer: Lord! Make me relevant in my endeavors!

June 11th

[ONE YEAR BIBLE PLAN: Ezra 1-2/ John 19:23-42]

WORD SWORD OF THE ORACLE

Today's Word: Esther 4:16

*"Go, gather all the Jews who are present in Shushan, and **fast** for me; neither eat nor drink for three days, night or day. My maids and I will fast likewise...."*

FASTING [HEBREW] 'TSUM'

'Tsum' is the Hebrew word for 'fasting' as used above and in [2 Samuel 12:23] Strong's #6684. The root word simply means "to abstain from food." At times fasting meant abstaining from: drinking, bathing, anointing with oil, or sexual intercourse as well. In essence, fasting acknowledges human frailty before God and appeals to His mercy. Fasting was a common practice in the ancient world, associated with mourning the dead [2 Samuel 12:21-22], intercessory prayer [Esther 4:3, Esther 4:16], repentance and contrition for sin [Jeremiah 36:9, Jonah 3:5], and times of distress [Judges 20:26, Nehemiah 1:4]. Fasting was required for the Day of Atonement ['affliction of your soul'] [Leviticus 16:31].

There were also four fast days that commemorated the destruction of Jerusalem by the Babylonians [Zechariah 8:19]. Fast varied in length from one day [1 Samuel 14:24, Daniel 6:18] to seven days [1 Samuel 31:13] and could even last for forty days on extraordinary occasions [Exodus 34:28]. The strict fast lasted from sunrise to sunset. But no matter what type of fasting was performed, the prophet Isaiah admonished his people to participate in acts of righteousness and social justice with their fasting [Isaiah 58:3-9].

Second Sunday of the Month of June

[ONE YEAR BIBLE PLAN: Ezra 3-5/ John 20]

CHURCH AND HOME SUNDAY SCHOOL

WHAT HAPPENS TO MAN WHEN HE DIES?

When we die our spirit returns to God and the body falls into the sleep of death. The flesh decays and returns to dust, but the seed of the body lies dormant [sleeps] awaiting resurrection.

Job 14:14 *"If a man dies, shall he live again? All the days of my hard service I will wait, till my change comes."*

Ecclesiastes 12:7 *"Then the dust will return to the earth as it was, and the spirit will return to God who gave it."*

1 Corinthians 15:35-38 *"But someone will say, "How are the dead raised up? And with what body do they come?" Foolish one, what you sow is not made alive unless it dies. And what you sow, you do not sow that body that shall be, but mere grain—perhaps wheat or some other grain. But God gives it a body as He pleases, and to each seeds its own body."*

1 Corinthians 15:42 *"So also is the resurrection of the dead. The body is sown in corruption, it is raised in incorruption."*

Sunday School Question

1) What happens to man when he dies?

Memorize: 1 Corinthians 15:42 "So also is the resurrection of the dead. The body is sown in corruption, it is raised in incorruption."

June 13th

[ONE YEAR BIBLE PLAN: Ezra 6-8/ John 21]

Today's Word: Exodus 14:11-22

THE BARRIER TO MY PROGRESS IS REMOVED!

Exodus 14:11-12 *".... For it would have been better for us to serve the Egyptians than that we should die in the wilderness."* Humans are the same; no matter the country, race, age, dispensation etc. Their reactions to situations are always the same. The Israelites rejoice when God delivered them from the captivity of Egypt and with the spoiling of their captors they were over joyous [Exodus 12:33-36]. But as they encounter barriers on their way to the Land of Promise, they began to complain against Moses and God as they see the chariots of Pharaoh racing towards them and the Red Sea ahead of them. Many times when faced with difficulties, we tend to react like the Israelites in our text-passage above. Some give up on life's pursuit because of oppositions. Others compromise their stands, while others make do with little successes for fear of challenges on the way to greatness.

Such should not be the reaction of Believers; that is why God berated Moses and the Israelites in [Exodus 14:15]. And He instructed them to move forward and as they did, the Red Sea parted before them. Likewise, God expects us to face life's challenges with faith in His ability to deliver us. Are you up against a barrier? Just brace up and begin to advance believing that God will miraculously make a way for you! And I decree every barrier to your progress shall give way!

Prayer: Lord! Grant me the grace to move boldly against every barrier in my way to success in Jesus' name. Amen!

June 14th

[ONE YEAR BIBLE PLAN: Ezra 9-10/ Acts 1]

Today's Word: Romans 4:19-20

MY WEAK FAITH SHALL BECOME STRONG!

Faith comes by hearing God's Word again and again [Romans 10:17]. This means that the more of God's Word you hear, the greater your faith becomes. Yet, it is possible to have a lot of faith that isn't strong. It is like a person who eats a lot until he/she gets so massive; yet does little or no exercises.

All he has is a lot of fat and flesh that is weak and soft. A smaller person who is fit and well-toned may undo him effortlessly, because even though he's big, he is weak. So, weak faith is the result of lack of exercise of faith, or the non-exercise of faith. If you hear the Word of God, but you don't act on it, your faith will be weak. This is the reason it is possible to know all the verses in the bible concerning a subject and yet have no result.

Until you act on the Word, you will receive nothing from the Word. Your faith remains weak and you will stagger when storms of life come. But the moment you decide to exercise your faith, by putting the Word to work, your faith will be strong. Abraham had strong faith! He called himself father of many even when he had no descendants yet. The Bible say he was "strong in faith, giving glory to God" and that's one characteristic of strong faith: strong faith gives glory to God by declaring that God has done whatever He says He will do! When your faith is strong, you readily accept, believe and do whatever God tells you in His Word. Amen!

June 15th

[ONE YEAR BIBLE PLAN: Nehemiah 1-3/ Acts 2:1-21

Today's Word: Lamentations 3:21-24

GOD'S FAITHFULNESS SHALL MANIFEST IN ME!

2 Timothy 2:13 says if we believe not, yet he abideth faithful: he cannot deny himself. Romans 3:4 says God forbid: yea let God be true, but every man a liar..." Numbers 23:19 says God is not a man, that he should lie; neither the son of man, that he should repent: hath he said, and shall he not do it? Or hath he spoken, and shall he not make it good? 2 Corinthians 1:20 says for all the promises of God in him are yea, and Amen, unto the glory of God by us." Alleluia!

"Years ago there is this testimony of a sister who came to our meeting and the Word of God came and said there is someone here who applied for visa, it is already done. She said Amen and was happy. She went to the embassy the next day. On arrival, the visa officer inspected her documents and declined the application and the sister said, but my pastor said it is done. The consular officer looked at her and said; who is your pastor? And she said my father is the Oracle. Then the visa officer answered and said even if your father is a Minister, a Governor, or a Commissioner, or the Pope get out now before I call security. As the sister turned reluctantly to go, she said but God said I have been granted visa, at that point the officer said, because you are so naive and funny, I will give you the visa. Glory to God! God has spoken it is already settled." I Prophesy to you now, the Lord will speak favorably concerning you in Jesus' name. Amen!

Prayer: Lord! Let Your faithfulness speak well to my destiny!

June 16th

[ONE YEAR BIBLE PLAN: Nehemiah 4-6/ Acts 2:22-47]

Today's Word: Romans 2:13, James 1:19-25

I AM A HEARER AND DOER OF GOD'S WORD!

There are two kinds of Believers: the 'hearers only' and the 'hearer and doers.' You belong to one of them. Many spend time listening to sermons on CDs, DVDs, TVs, direct messages in the church and spend much more time studying the Bible. Which is very good; however, this may not get you any result without doing what you learn. Joshua was given the secret to success by God in [Joshua 1:8]. This verse simply says; unless you walk in total obedience and submission to God's Word, there is no guarantee of good success in life.

When you hear or read the Scriptures, it stays, in your head. If left there for a while, without taking further steps, the birds of the air will come and steal it. If you desire that the Word make a meaningful impact in your life, then you must make the extra effort to transfer it from your head into your heart – your spirit man: [Romans 12:2]. You must fill your heart and actively occupy it with the Word, so that when tempted, the Word of God will spill out of you: '... for out of the abundance of the heart the month speaks. The Psalmist says: "Thy words have I hid in my heart that I might not sin against Thee." Give valuable time to meditating on the Word you've heard. You will find it easy and very compelling to obey the Word after you've meditated on it.

Thinking upon the Word leads you on a journey into further revelations. When you put what you have heard or read into practice, success results. Cultivate the habit of doing the Word. Remain Blessed!

June 17th

[ONE YEAR BIBLE PLAN: Nehemiah 7-9/ Acts 3]

Today's Word: Nahum 1:9

I DECREE! AN END TO ALL MY AFFLICTIONS!

The following praise report will surely edify you so read on:
".....when the usher that was serving my row with the Holy Communion passed me by; I knew that the enemy wanted to deny me of my miracle. I had to step out of line to ask another usher to serve me. Immediately, I took the bread and wine, [the Body and Blood of Jesus] my stomach started bubbling. I belched continuously as bubbles of gas rose up my system and escaped through the mouth. When I got home that day; I noticed that the offensive odor that usually emanate from my private part ceased. I then went for a test which revealed that the disease had completely disappeared. Glory to God!
Sister Janice NJ.

This sister have been tormented by demonic affliction for many years; and she had several modern medical test and treatment with no result; she went from one prayer house to another to no avail; she used all kinds of herbs none brought her any succor. She continued in her pain and shame until she partook in the Holy Communion in our meeting and got delivered her! Glory to God!

Saint! Are you afflicted, discouraged and down cast? Rejoice this day because by the power in the Blood of Jesus Christ; the Son of the Living God; that affliction is destroyed now in Jesus' name! I decree an end to all the afflictions in your life in the name of Jesus. Amen!

June 18th

[ONE YEAR BIBLE PLAN: Nehemiah 10-11/ Acts 4:1-22]

Today's Word: Esther 3:7

"In the first month, which is the month of Nisan, in the twelfth year of King Ahasuerus, they cast Pur (that is, the lot), before Haman to determine the day and the month, until it fell on the twelfth month, which is the month of Adar."

LOT [HEBREW] 'PUR'

The Hebrew word for 'Lot' is 'Pur' as used in our text-verse above and also in [Esther 9:24; Esther 9:26] Strong's Concordance #6332: The Hebrew word is originally a Babylonian word meaning "lot" or "fate," and is used in the Book of Esther as a synonym for the normal Hebrew word for "lot." Lot casting, which is similar to rolling dice; was a common way to decide or make random selection [Nehemiah 11:1]. Or to discern the will of a god [Jonah 1:7] Believing that his gods controlled the fall of Pur, Haman cast lots to determine the right day to destroy the Jews in Shushan [Esther 3:7]. What he failed to realize was that God is sovereign and cannot be manipulated by superstition [Proverbs 16:33].

By casting lots, Haman inadvertently chose the day of the Jews' deliverance: a day that is still celebrated in the land of Israel as the festival of Purim [Esther 9:28].

Prayer: Father Lord! Turn the plans of my enemies against them in Jesus' name. Amen!

Third Sunday of the Month of June

[ONE YEAR BIBLE PLAN: Nehemiah 12-13/ Acts 4:23-37]

CHURCH AND HOME SUNDAY SCHOOL

How many resurrections will be there?

here will be two resurrections: the resurrection of the dead in Christ and the resurrection of the wicked.

1 Corinthians 15:51-52 *"Behold, I tell you a mystery: We shall not all sleep, but we shall all be changed— in a moment, in the twinkling of an eye, at the last trumpet. For the trumpet will sound, and the dead will be raised incorruptible, and we shall be changed."*

Revelation 20:5-6 *"But the rest of the dead did not live again until the thousand years were finished. This is the first resurrection. 6 Blessed and holy is he who has part in the first resurrection. Over such the second death has no power, but they shall be priests of God and of Christ, and shall reign with Him a thousand years."*

John 5:28-29 *"Do not marvel at this; for the hour is coming in which all who are in the graves will hear His voice 29 and come forth— those who have done good, to the resurrection of life, and those who have done evil, to the resurrection of condemnation."*

Sunday School Question

1) How many resurrections will be there?

Memory Verse: John 11:25 "Jesus said to her, "I am the resurrection and the life. He who believes in Me, though he may die, he shall live."

June 20th

[ONE YEAR BIBLE PLAN: Esther 1-2/ Acts 5:1-21]

Today's Word: Matthew 17:24-27

YHE LORD GOD WILL PROVIDE FOR ME FROM UNCOMMON SOURCE!

Matthew 17:27, *"..... Notwithstanding, lest we should offend them, go thou to the sea, and cast an hook, and take up the fish that first cometh up; and when thou hast opened his mouth, thou shalt find a piece of money: that take, and give unto them for me and thee."* The story above says one day the tax master asked Peter; what about the tax for your master Jesus? So, Jesus said to Peter, in order not to offend them, go to the river, cast your hook, and the first fish you catch, open its mouth; there will be a gold coin therein, take it and use it to pay for you and for me.

Everyone knows that fish don't eat metal but when God commands a fish to swallow gold coin it obeys. Much more than that, when God commands a fish and says, a hook is coming, you must be the first one to swallow the hook, the fish obeys. I am telling you this because there is a river in your city of abode containing a fish and in the mouth of that fish is your financial breakthrough; very soon you will catch that fish, as you start and continue to fish for souls, as you start winning people to Christ, the one who has your money in his/her mouth will be born again in Jesus' name! And that person will link you to your financial breakthrough in Jesus' name. Amen!

Prayer: Lord! Give me the grace to evangelize, in Jesus' name. Amen!

June 21st

[ONE YEAR BIBLE PLAN: Esther 3-5/ Acts 5:22-42]

Today's Word: 2 Chronicles 25:1-2

I DECLARE! THE LORD WILL FIND ME BLAMELESS!

David understood the importance of the heart in God's evaluation that is why he said in Psalm 51:10 *"Create in me a clean heart, O God, and renew a steadfast spirit within me."*

Why you do a thing; is more important to God than what you do. This is so because, whereas men look at the exterior; God looks inwardly at the heart. That is why David was chosen King over his brethren [1 Samuel 16:7]. That also, was why Solomon became the wisest and the wealthiest king of his time [2 Chronicles 1:11]. So we can't impress or influence God with works but with faith. [Hebrews 11:6]. God can't be fooled! He searches out the heart for motives. Selfishness is unacceptable to Him. In his book "The Final Quest" Rick Joyner surmised that man can reform the whole world and yet lose his or her soul. In our text-passage, King Amaziah took several decisions as king of Judah that was right. But as far as God is concern, Amaziah was not righteous because his motive did not meet God's standard.

Saint! I may not know the decisions you make and take in life; but if you only seek God when you are in need, know now that God knows your motive and will recompense according to your motive. I pray that God will find you blameless in Jesus' name. Amen!

Prayer: Lord! Create in me a clean heart this day in the name of Jesus. Amen!

June 22nd

[ONE YEAR BIBLE PLAN: Esther 6-8/ Acts 6]

Today's Word: 2 Chronicles 23:1-15

EVIL POWER HINDERING MY TESTIMONY IS SLAIN!

When Athaliah forcefully took over the throne of Judah in [2 Chr. 22:10-12], she violated God's Covenant with David: that the seed of David shall forever be on the throne. [2 Chr. 23:3]. By so doing, she stood between Joash and the throne that was his; by Covenant right. For six years, she perpetuated this anomaly until God raised Jehoiada to dislodge her. With the help of God; Jehoiada slew her and enthroned Joash as the rightful king over Judah. There are many 'Athaliahs' in this day and age. They forcefully snatch position and properties from rightful owners. Where such powers operate, they try, just like Athaliah did, to annihilate the rightful owner[s] of positions and/or properties. But when God's power is brought to bear in such situations; opposition are dislodged and destroyed and God's children can enjoy their blessings and the name of the Lord is glorified. Are you in the position Joash found himself? Has the 'Athaliah' of your family withstood the promises of God in your life? I decree this day, every power hindering God's promises in your life is slain in Jesus' name! I invoke the power in the Word of God which is a double edged sword to slay your enemies in Jesus' name. Now you must arise and use the sword of the Spirit and slain every 'Athaliah' in your life in Jesus' name. As you do so, the angel that is assign by God to this ministry will arise and fight for you in Jesus' name. Amen!

Prayer: Every power hindering my blessings is slain now!

June 23rd

[ONE YEAR BIBLE PLAN: Esther 9-10/ Acts 7:1-21]

Today's Word: Mark 11:23

I DECLARE! MY SICK FIATH IS CURED!

I am amazed at what many believers declare from God's Word, without acting on it. For instance, a Believer says "I know the Bible says "by His stripe I am healed" but he/she is lying down sick. That is weak faith or a 'sick faith' so to say. Weak faith is the result of 'lack of exercise' of faith; the result of not acting on the information you have received from the Word of God.

It is like a person who keeps eating but does no exercise; his muscles will grow big but very weak. In the same vein, God's Word is food to your spirit. If you keep receiving God's Word and do nothing with it, your faith will be weak. Weak faith causes you to stagger, and as a result, fear creeps in and grips you; then you are overwhelmed and defeated by the crisis of life! The cure for a sick or weak faith is acting on God's Word; by acting on the information you've received. If you want your faith to be great and do great things for you, start doing the Word! [1 Thessalonians 5:16] says put this to work in your life, work the Word and the Word will work for you. Give thanks in all situations; let your life be an unending stream of praise and thanksgiving to the Lord. Tell yourself I refuse to be sick! Always say, I refuse to lie down on the sick bed or remain in the wheelchair or go about with crutches for I am healed of the Lord. Alleluia!

Prayer: Lord! Heal my sick faith in the name of Jesus. Amen!

June 24th

[ONE YEAR BIBLE PLAN: Job 1-2/ Acts 7:22-43]

Today's Word: Psalm 90:1-6

THE PROTECTIVE ARMOR OF GOD IS OVER ME!

Smart people protect themselves, their loved ones and their property from preventable tragedies. The things of the Lord also need to be protected. As you endeavor to zealously preserve and protect the things of God; He will do great things in your life. However, when good things happen, we need to protect them ourselves. When your house is full of treasures, you've to guard it, Proverbs 1:32 says: *"The prosperity of fools shall be their destruction."* No doubt you are going to prosper, but you should not let your prosperity destroy you. For your prosperity not to destroy you; you must put on the whole Armor of God; which is His provision for your protection. If you fail to use it and the enemy succeeds in attacking you; the fault is yours. You must not blame God. So to render the attack of the enemy on you ineffective, the onus is on you to put on the Whole Armor of God.

If you find that in spite of all the promises of God, the enemy still penetrates, and you are still the tail and not the head, and poverty is overtaking you, then you should ask yourself some questions. You should ask whether you have on; the whole Armor of God. You should examine yourself for God is not a failure. He is not a liar. He will perform whatever He promises. God wants you to be victorious all the time. He said we should put on the Whole Armor of God to be able to withstand in the evil day. Having done this, we must still be on our feet standing!

June 25th

[ONE YEAR BIBLE PLAN: Job 3-4/ Acts 7:44-60]

WORD SWORD OF THE ORACLE

Today's Word: Job 1:1

*"There was a man in the land of Uz, whose name was Job; and that man was **blameless** and upright, and one who feared God and shunned evil."*

BLAMELESS [HEBREW] 'TAM'

The Hebrew word 'Tam' is translated 'blameless' as used in the above text-verse and also in [Job 1:8; Job 8:20; Job 9:21; Psalm 37:37] Strong's Concordance #8535:

The verbal root of this Hebrew word means "to be complete." Thus, this word signifies an individual's integrity- "a wholeness and wholesomeness." The word is used as a term of endearment for the Shulamite bride in Songs of Solomon, see 'perfect' in [Songs of Solomon chapter number 5 and verse 2; Song of Solomon 6:9].

In the Old Testament, the blameless are frequently associated with the upright [Job 1:1; Job 1:8; Job 2:3; Psalm 37:37; Proverbs 29:10] and contrasted with the wicked [Job 9:22; Psalm 64:2-4].

Job's claim to be blameless agrees with God's assessment of him, but it is not a claim to be absolute perfection [Job 1:8; Job 9:21; Job 14:16-17]. The Psalmist writes that the future of the blameless man is peace as was the case for Job in [Job 42:10-12; Psalm 37:37].

Prayer: Father! Give me the grace to be blameless in the name of Jesus. Amen!

Fourth Sunday of the Month of June

[ONE YEAR BIBLE PLAN: Job 5-7/ Acts 8:1-25]

CHURCH AND HOME SUNDAY SCHOOL

Is the soul conscious after death?

Yes! Jesus taught that Lazarus and the rich man were conscious, had memory and faculties of expression. Luke 16:19-31 *"...So it was that the beggar died, and was carried by the angels to Abraham's bosom. The rich man also died and was buried. And being in torments in Hades, he lifted up his eyes and saw Abraham afar off and Lazarus in his bosom. "Then he cried and said, 'Father Abraham, have mercy on me, and send Lazarus that he may dip the tip of his finger in water and cool my tongue; for I am tormented in this flame..."*

1 Peter 3:19 *"by whom also He went and preached to the spirits in prison."*

IS THERE RECOGNITION OF LOVED ONES AFTER DEATH?

Yes! The dead in paradise and in sheol-Hades recognized those whom they knew on earth. Matthew 8:11 *"And I say to you that many will come from east and west, and sit down with Abraham, Isaac, and Jacob in the kingdom of heaven."*

Sunday School Question

1) Is the soul conscious after death?
2) Is there recognition of loved ones after death?

Memory Verse: Luke 16:31 "But he said to him, 'If they do not hear Moses and the prophets, neither will they be persuaded though one rise from the dead.'"

June 27th

[ONE YEAR BIBLE PLAN: Job 8-10/ Acts 8:26-40]

Today's Word: Psalm 40:2-4

GOD SHALL TURN MY CRIES TO SMILES!

This testimony will help build your faith read on: *"I came back from Nigeria, to the US early last year with two 40 ft containers load of produce. I could not clear the container from the port due to custom duties and all sorts of regulations. In the process of time after incurring unbelievable storages fee and charges, I was able to raise enough money to get one of the containers out of the port. I could not clear the other container until the God of the Oracle intervened. My wife and I met with the man of God after one of the miracle conventions. On narrating our ordeal, he placed us on a 7 day fast with some scriptures to use and he declared: on or before the end of the fast the container is released. Even though I said Amen, I did not believe it was possible, because of what I had gone through at the customs. But lo and behold, to my greatest and pleasant surprise on the third day of the fast the container was released with a letter of apology because the authority had overcharged my containers, and as a result they are sending me a refund of $3,700.59 for excess storage charges and other compensations."* Glory to God! Brother Femi; Baltimore MD.

Are you financially stuck? Has the enemy seized your testimonies? Is your happiness hindered by people? The Lord is taking you out of that struggle now and He is turning your cries to smiles this day in Jesus' name. Amen!

Prayer: Lord, divinely favor with all men in Jesus' name!

June 28th

[ONE YEAR BIBLE PLAN: Job 11-13/ Acts 9:1-21]

Today's Word: Isaiah 48:18

I DECREE! MY PEACE SHALL BE LIKE A RIVER!

In the text verse above, God is saying if only you listened attentively to my commandments then your peace would've been like a river and your righteousness as the waves of the sea. Anytime you hear the word 'storm'; a picture goes through your mind: picture of disturbance, picture of trouble, picture of unpleasant things. But when you hear the word 'peace'; you have a different picture; of pleasant things, restfulness, everything harmonious. So storm stands for; trouble, unpleasant things, lack of rest. And peace stands for; harmony, rest. Which is why Jesus is called the Prince of peace [Isaiah 9:6]; and He has the ability to still every storm in your life.

In [Mark 4:35-41] there was a storm and Jesus was sleeping and they woke Him up; He spoke and said 'Peace Be Still' and calmed the storm. And they said "what manner of man is this, that the wind and the sea obeyed Him?" I pray that the Prince of peace will calm every storm in your life this day in the name of Jesus. Are you going through a storm? I decree! Peace that flows like a river in your life in the name of Jesus! Do you need spiritual or physical peace? Receive it now in Jesus' name! Do you really desire this kind of overflowing peace? [Isaiah 48:18] says you must obey God's commandments then your peace shall be like a river and your righteousness as the waves of the sea. Alleluia!

Prayer: Lord! Give me the grace to obey you in Jesus' name!

June 29th

[ONE YEAR BIBLE PLAN: Job 14-16/ Acts 9:22-43]

Today's Word: John 6:1-6:13

DIVINE ENCOUNTER IS MINE AS I GIVE THANKS

A spirit of thanksgiving brings uncommon blessings. [John 6:11] says "Then Jesus took the loaves, gave thanks to God, and passed them out to the people. Afterward he did the same with the fish. And they all ate until they were full". This miracle of multiplication is a result of the natural manifesting the supernatural through thanksgiving. But it will only happen as you give quality appreciation to God. It takes knowledge to acknowledge God's faithfulness. It takes faith and grace to have a sincere attitude of gratitude; but God rewards our faith with grace by doing more than we could ever imagine possible. God is working everything together for your good, no matter what the situation may be, you must have faith. And as you respond to God with thanksgiving, no matter your circumstance, you'll see the fruition of your expectations; as your blessings become a reality. This was the attitude of Paul and Silas when they were jailed in Philippi in [Acts 16:25-26].

PRAYER OF THANKS:

Thank You Jesus, for taking me through January from April to through June. Thank You Father for; You who began a good work in me, will perfect it until the day of Jesus Christ. Thank You for bring me thus far. I thank You for daily signs and wonders, thank You Lord for provision, preservation and protection. Thank You Lord for there is no one like You, king of Glory, take all the glory, in Jesus name I have given thanks. Amen!

June 30th

[ONE YEAR BIBLE PLAN: Job 17-19/ Acts 10:1-23]

Today's Word: Psalm 16:11

"You will show me the path of life; in Your presence is fullness of joy; at Your right hand are pleasures forevermore."

MY REPETANCE SHALL TURN MY SORROW TO JOY!

God is Holy and he says be ye holy. You can't experience fullness of joy and the pleasure of God when you dwell in iniquity, because sin will chase God away from you and your prayers becomes abomination unto Him. But, on repentance your joy shall be full. I know it is possible for you to be saved today, because the blood of Jesus Christ that cleanses from all sins has not lost His power.

And it is also possible for you to be baptized in the Holy Ghost right now? Because the Almighty God declared that the promise is for you. And He says you shall receive power when the Holy Ghost is come upon you [Acts 1:8]. Absolutely victory will be yours today, because if God be for you, no one can be against you. If you don't accept Him on visitation, God won't force you. When the messenger got to the field and said to David, you are wanted at home. If David had said don't bother me, I am enjoying myself here with the sheep in [1 Samuel 16]; that would have been the end of the story of David becoming a King. But if you come to God now, this can be the beginning of your celebration. So, if you want to give your life to Christ pray this prayer now.

Prayer: Begin to ask God to forgive all your sins, ask Him to wash you clean in His blood, tell Him you will serve Him for the rest of your life. Tell Him to save your soul now*!*

SALVATION PRAYER

Dear Father,

I come to You in the Name of Jesus. Your Word says in John 6:37 *"...him that cometh to me, I will in no wise cast out"*.

I thank You for not casting me out. I thank You for drawing me onto You, I surrender my life to You today and I confess with my mouth that Jesus Christ is Lord and I believe with my heart that you raised Him from the dead. I ask that the blood of Jesus cleanse me from all my sin and deliver me from all my iniquity Thank You Lord for saving me. Father, please write my name in the book of life in Jesus name I pray. Amen

Heavens are rejoicing this day for your sake.

Name: ....

Address: ....

....

Contact number: ....

Date: ....

JOIN OUR PROPHETIC CONFERENCE

DIAL 712.432.0075 AND ENTER CODE 188641#

OR 30222021110 Enter code 605315

6AM AND 10 PM EST

MONDAYS THROUGH SATURDAYS; 5PM ONLY ON SUNDAYS.
CALL TOLL TO FREE TO ORDER FOR PRAYERS
1.800.481.3884 FAX PRAYERS TO 1.888. 413.5990

www.ooGod.org/pastor@oogod.org

donate@oracleofGodministries.net

WORSHIP WITH US
ORACLE OF GOD CHURCHES

MARYLAND

✏ 9470 Annapolis Rd
Ste 208, Lanham, Md 20706

NORTH CAROLINA

✏ 5731 New Bern Avenue,
Raleigh NC 27610 H/W 64 EAST

Write or Call us

ORACLE OF GOD INT'L MINISTRIES
An International full Gospel and Deliverance Prayer Ministry

POSTAL ADDRESS
P.O. BOX 14068 NC 27620
TEL: 1800.481.3884. FAX: 1888.413.5990

Pray with us

**PRAYER CONFERENCE: 267.507.0240
ENTER 605815
MONDAYS THROUGH SATURDAYS
@ 6 AM AND 10 PM EST**

log on

WWW.ORACLEOFGODMINISTRIES.NET/
DONATE@ORACLEOFGODMINISTRIES.NET

www.ingramcontent.com/pod-product-compliance
Lightning Source LLC
Chambersburg PA
CBHW052027070526
44584CB00016B/1941